Marriage
and the
Trifling
Things We Do!

Shirley Lytle

SkrAiber®
PUBLISHING SERVICES

Chandler, Arizona

MARRIAGE AND THE TRIFLING THINGS WE DO

Copyright © 2006 by Shirley E. Lytle
Of DSL Ministries: www.dslministries.org

Library of Congress Cataloging-In-Publication Data

Lytle, Shirley E.
Marriage and the trifling things we do / Shirley E. Lytle. – 1st ed.
p.   cm

Library of Congress Control Number: 2006931918

ISBN 10 0-9772099-2-X
ISBN 13 9780977209927
1.   Marriage – Christian Counselling
2.   Relationships – Couples
3.   Premarital – Christian Counselling

Cover Design by Bosgraphdesign

Printed in the United Status of the America

SkrAiber
PUBLISHING SERVICES

Chandler, Arizona 85249
www.skraiberpublishing.com

2006931918

Dedication

This book is dedicated to my husband, best friend and marriage ministry partner, Darryl Lytle. Darryl is the true king of our home and through his love and devotion DSL Ministries (www.dslministries.org) was born. Darryl, I love you!

Acknowledgements

I thank my parents, Nathaniel and Elaine Smith who encouraged me as a child that all things are possible with God at the helm.

To my son, David: I love and appreciate you for understanding how important it was for me to write this book.

To my baby brother, James, who will always be my lifelong coach.

To my prayer warriors, Joy and Felissa: Your intercessory prayers are felt daily.

To the couples Darryl and I counseled: Thank you for giving us the opportunity to share God's plan on how to celebrate your marriages!

To Skraiber Publishing and Fred Smith for believing this book is worth getting into the hands of those who need it.

Contents

Foreword

It is with great delight that I write the foreword to "Marriage and the Trifling Things We Do" a book that I believe is going to make a lasting impact on millions of married couples and those on the way to the altar.

There is no institution as foundational to a structured society as the institution of marriage and there is no other institution that is under such relentless attack. Satan, our common adversary has saved his most lethal weapons for the marital relationship. How else could he divert the destiny of so many or cause such great pain and paralysis. How else could he plant seeds that would infect and affect generations to come, other than through the institution of marriage?

We now live in a time where we are at war, in an attempt [some say], to bring liberty to the captives. However, I would suggest that in homes on every block of every city in this nation there are couples under all out attack, being held hostage by narrow vision, past hurtful relationships, and unrealistic expectations, trying to alter somebody they took to the altar.

Well, into this fight for marriages God has sent these seasoned veterans to speak words of life and hope. It has been my joy to have known Darryl and Shirley for nine years. Throughout those years I have entrusted them with the married couples in our ministry. As any Pastor will testify: We take great care

to inspect those who will speak into the lives of those we are called to lead. I have examined the work of this couple and found no fault. They not only have over 25 years of personal marital experience to their credit, but knowing that they were called to this work, they have studied to show themselves approved in this area. They both have a personal and growing relationship with the Lord, a sound understanding of the Word of God and a commitment to following pastoral leadership that is to be imitated.

As you read this book you will sense not just the academic discipline of this couple, but you will sense the fire, passion and sense of humor that really enables them to connect with couples at all phases of their relationship. In this book they take you through different stages in marital relationships and I believe you will feel the truth of the illustrations, and you might even find yourself in a few of them. Shirley takes the readers on a journey through trifling attitudes, beliefs, and behaviors but always end with the treasured responses that give light and lift to the relationship.

As you read you will find this book to be "full of grace and truth." It is delightfully hilarious, appropriately serious, and always faithful to scripture. As you read thoughtfully, I pray that you will be forever impacted.

Bishop Alexis Thomas
Senior Pastor, Pilgrim Rest Baptist Church
Phoenix, Arizona
Bishop for the State of Arizona
Full Gospel Baptist Church Fellowship, International

Dear God,

It's me again. Can you help me out with a few things?

Help me to talk right.
Help me to walk right.
Help me to live right.
Most importantly, help me to love right.

Introduction

Do you celebrate your marriage? Do you share the successes that you have experienced? If you don't, you should! If you do, continue! Your marriage should be celebrated! Every individual who has been in a relationship, engaged, and now married, will find a reflection of their marriage in the following pages. The purpose of this book is to show that marriages can work, even though many of us enter into relationships ill-prepared.

My husband and I have spent over 20 years providing pre-marital counseling to couples and enrichment support for married couples. In that span of time, we have heard more than our share of stories of how couples have used manipulation or domination to manage a relationship. Marriage can work if it is managed according to God's blueprint. A marriage has a higher success rate when it lines up with God's plan.

The pages in this book are examples of "trifling" acts we have helped couples work through. The examples are **"real"**, but the names have been changed to protect us from being beaten down! Without a change in behavior, marriages are headed for a continued downward trend. We have combined humor with reality in order for the "medicine" to go down easier. Without a serious shot in the arm about how we perceive marriage and the importance of the covenant

1

established with God, we will continue to see an increase in the divorce rate among bodies of believers.

Finally, Satan continues to strike the foundation of the Church. When he strikes the Church, he strikes marriages. When he strikes marriages, he strikes families. We must safeguard our families by safeguarding our marriages. If we can encourage one couple to communicate better, to live as one powerful force as Christ designed us in the garden, then we have accomplished our job. We believe in God-given practical application of the Word. Over the past 25 years of our marriage, the Lord has revealed many truths to us regarding relationships, marriage, and how Christians struggle in these areas. Our prayer is that through these pages God will be revealed and marriages will be healed. Our goal is to help you go from a "Trifling Act" to a "Treasured Response".

Why Trifling?

The word trifling is an interesting word. Webster's Dictionary states that this word can be used as an adjective, a verb and a noun. Trifling has a connotation of negligible, inactivity, frivolous, or to act, perform or speak with little seriousness, slight worth or importance or purpose. Somewhere in the above definition lies the root of why our relationships are failing each and every day.

For the purpose of this book, I will use the word trifling as a verb.

Trifling: **An act which demonstrates the lack of importance or seriousness placed on the institution of marriage.**

We will explore some of the actions which affect how we meet, how we marry and how we get into trouble (ultimately a great deal of trouble we will see). Why? It is because our priorities are distorted and we are trifling. But have no fear; we will also discuss the magnificent power derived from living and loving God's way. My friends tease me about the metaphors that I live by each day. Mixing humor with realism seems to help others grasp concepts that the mind finds difficult to understand. From "you're trifling and you know it!" to "rise up from your oppression!" I find that these examples invoke an immediate visual of the current condition of a relationship.

However, the question might still loom: Why another book on marriage? Good question. The answer is that the *average* couple at some point needs a little help. The *average* person will go to the church for help and will not get the help they need. The *average* Christian will suffer in silence and then divorce in disgrace or denial without seeking out support. The *average* church struggles to keep up with the needs of Christian couples. The church is aware of the problems, but struggles to get a hold on how to effectively make an impact in order to promote change. When we fail to seek out wise counsel and wait until the relationship is broken and bleeding, we are committing a trifling act. We need open and honest discussions of how to make the "Word alive" in our marriages. It is important to discover what God would have you learn through your relationship with your spouse.

Making the Word alive in our relationships starts with believing in the deity of God. *Deuteronomy 28:13* states that the Lord has made us the head and not the tail. We are to be above and not beneath our circumstances. We are to behave in a manner that is of God and be in line with the written command-ments. The entire 28th chapter of Deuteronomy speaks of the covenant God has promised to His people! Following God's ways will guide you to walk in His likeness instead of the world's likeness. Through the power of God, we have dominion over our life. As the head, we are to listen with compassion, discernment and understanding. Words of encouragement, speak-ing with integrity and clarification with the right intentions should be seen and felt by all.

What a profound revelation to be directed by God's spoken Word. So, if indeed we are to be the head, why do we behave like the "tail end of a donkey's behind?" Because, we're **trifling!** Everyone can see that your "don't care meter" is in the red. Your actions exemplify a careless attitude about your marriage. Society has become accustomed to trading in things. Divorce is breaking down the church infrastructure. If your spouse does not act right, just trade him or her in for another model. In order for this and future generations to know the love of God, our mentality about divorce and marriage must move past trifling acts to treasured responses.

Trifling Act Scene 1:
Let's Play the Fig Leaf Game

From the fall of Adam and Eve, men and women have struggled with exposing their imperfections. Not only did Adam and Eve hide themselves from God with their fig leaves, they also hid themselves from each other. The *Fig Leaf* game we play accounts for so many of the problems we face in our marriages. The game combines intrigue, deception and denial.

The best *Fig leaf* game played today is called "Dating". It is the biggest cover up known to mankind, especially in the church. You are still covering up your issues in order to represent what you think others want to see.

The rules of the Fig Leaf Game

- First meet someone you are attracted to physically and/or intellectually.
- Find out what you think they like and dislike.
- Only show them the best you have to offer.
- Don't tell them about the issues you have with your parents, past relationships or struggles.
- Let them believe that everything about your past has been completely resolved. Give them the impression that the issues will never return and affect your future.
- Spend 6 months planning the wedding.

- Have one pre-marital counseling session with the minister.
- Get married.
- Wake up one morning and find out that the person you married is nothing like you thought.
- Off comes the fig leaf.
- Out come the excuses and disappointments.
- Game over.
- Fighting begins.

The goal should be to never start the game in a relationship in the first place. I agree it is important that you put your best foot forward when dating someone. Yet, don't forget that honesty and openness are important characteristics to have in a marriage. These characteristics seem to disappear, however, during the dating period. For example, learning that the man you just married does not want children and you do is not a good start. Telling yourself that he never showed you any signs that he did not want children while you were dating would be called "blind love" or "denial". If and when you date someone long enough, the true person shows up, which allows time for the Holy Spirit to provide discernment in your lives.

It is all in the cover up!

Take Stephanie and Jeffrey who were married two years ago. Stephanie agrees to meet me at one of my favorite breakfast spots for a discussion. Stephanie states she cannot understand why Jeffrey has suddenly changed. He is not acting anything like he used to when they were dating. I asked her how long they dated before marrying. Stephanie states boldly, "We dated for a good year, before we moved in with each other and planned the wedding". I asked her what the problem was. "Well", stated Stephanie, "He does not want anything to do with my family so I hardly get to see my mother anymore!" Over the next 15 minutes, she complains and cries about the birthday parties and family gatherings she has missed over the past year and a half. As Stephanie evaluated her short dating period, she acknowledged that her interaction with his family was limited. On the few occasions when there was a connection with his family the conversations seemed strained and distant.

On the other hand, when connecting with her family, Jeffrey seemed to admire the family bond. Additionally, Stephanie proceeded to tell me that what she admired most about Jeffrey while they were dating, was that Jeffrey spent most holidays with her and her family. She thought it was sweet that he would "give up" his family time to be with her. How sweet...not really, just trifling. She admits the topic of how they would deal with in-laws was never discussed before they married.

Jeffrey gave her all the signs in the world, but she was blinded by the physical, which kept her from seeking out the spiritual aspects of the relationship. A spirit of discernment will alert you to issues that require attention. Now they have a situation to address. The Lord will give us the signs. "Beware...she wants children!" "He does not know how to spell JOB, let alone keep one." "She is high maintenance and does not know how to budget.", "He spells submission, SUBJECTION". These are just a few signs that take the fig leaf off the person. You are too busy trying to explain them away instead of finding out what God is trying to teach you from the dating experience.

Before I make this statement understand that I am a visual individual, so I describe situations and narrate opportunities in a visual way. Many times when I am speaking to people, I find it necessary to go visual when the intellectual is not hitting the point effectively. With that being said....people when you are looking for a mate, do not get **blinded by the behind, the booty**, etc. You get the point. When the physical appearances are your primary prerequisite for your soul mate, you have missed the mark and reduced your future to one trifling act of lust. Breasts, hair and physique will pass away but the Word of God endures forever. Lasting love goes beyond physical and financial profiles. God's love demonstrates long suffering, kindness, patience and mercy on a regular basis. When you demonstrate God's love in your marriage, you release His power into your situation.

From a Trifling Act to a Treasured Response: Acts 27:10

Playing the Fig leaf game will cause storms to rise up in your marriage. Many couples have played the cover up game for so long that they do not know where the truth starts and the lie begins. This is why premarital counseling and marriage enrichment programs are important. In *Acts 27:10* Paul attempts to advise the folks on the boat that the trip ahead will be dangerous and will have potential fatalities. No one would listen to Paul. The difficult truth of the matter is that regardless of how much counseling you extend to a couple, most refuse to believe the advice will have relevance to their situation. Regardless of whether the couple is young and never married or this is the second or third time around and in the prime of their lives, some folks just do not want to embrace changing their thought process. So here are few questions to make you think.

1. What are your strengths and what are your weaknesses?
2. Have you identified that your weaknesses are strengths to your spouse?
3. What is God trying to teach you about yourself through your spouse?
4. Have you forgiven each other for playing games before you were married?

Trifling Act Scene 2: Two edged sword

Trifling stuff happens when you attempt to hold your spouse to one standard and you do not hold yourself to the same standard. For example the double standard states that your husband can go out and have a great time with his co-workers without you. However, your wife must secure her husband's permission in order to go out with her friends.   Another example is: You will use your money any kind of way you want to. However your spouse must use his or her money to pay all the bills. At some point the two-edged sword will turn on you and then what do you do? Will you ask for mercy, the same mercy that your trifling self could not give to your spouse? Let's take a look at a typical issue most couples deal with.

The Sword Game

Eddie works for a mid-size company; he has made a point to omit any communication regarding his spouse other than to state he is married. Eddie just received an email about an after work happy hour celebration for one of his peers. He wants to have a great time without Amy! He believes she brings him down in public and he cannot be himself when she is around. So what does Eddie do? He lies about the event. He tells Amy that he is required to attend the function and that spouses are not invited. Amy has asked time after time why Eddie's company is anti-family. Oh, by the way, Eddie has omitted the fact that the celebration is for Candice, one of the single employees from work.

Amy begins to interrogate Eddie about the details of the function. Eddie gets defensive and states that she is getting on his nerves and is clingy. He continues to rant and rave that he does not know why she wants to go when she will not know anyone. Finally, he pulls the "head of the house" card and states he will be going and she will stay home. Amy feels betrayed and believes Eddie is out of order and dishonoring her by socializing with other females after work hours. For those of you who are unsure of whether Eddie is wrong – he is!

One month later, Amy has an opportunity to go out of town for a girl's weekend. Amy has a free ticket and really needs to be around other Christian married women. She asks Eddie if it is ok for her go. Eddie rants and raves about the cost of the trip and that they do not have the money. Amy responds by stating that her friends are pitching in to pay for the trip so there are no out of pocket costs for her. Eddie has the nerve to ask who is going to take care of the house work while she is gone for 3 days. It is interesting now that the shoe is on the other foot that Eddie is struggling to find ways to manipulate the situation to get his way. Now who is going to be left home alone?

Out of respect for her husband, Amy says, "I won't go, if you don't want me to." Eddie then throws out the religion card. "It would not be appropriate for you to go out of town without your husband, but you may go if you want to." Amy is confused as to why Eddie is

12

against her cost-free trip. Is it possible that Eddie believes he has lost this round of manipulation and does not want to concede defeat? Eddie has fallen on his sword and the situation is bleeding without a bandage to be found. Why didn't Eddie consider his inappropriate behavior when the happy hour incident occurred? What is just as troubling is that Amy feels guilty for challenging her husband's decision...which is her job as a help-mate.

It amazes me how holy we become when it is comfortable for us. It is amazing how we will use scripture to justify our actions. This gross misuse of the Word can only result in distorting God's image and God exposing you for the trifling individual you really are. Allow the Word of God (The Sword) to convict your actions, and walk in a manner that honors God and your spouse.

Eddie spent too much time trying to get his way instead of trying to understand his spouse. He has enforced a level of power in the relationship that exploits his wife's weak areas. There can be no honor in taking advantage of someone who places his or her trust in you. Funny how you cannot be yourself or be responsible when it matters the most. You lose your witness of how good God is when you fail to represent your household in an appropriate manner.

Life is more than getting your way. Life is strengthened by feeding one another to the degree that he or she can stand on their own. When you build up your spouse in all places instead of tearing him or her down, you bring out their potential. Allow the sword to cut off those things in your life that are weighing you down. Encourage your spouse to concentrate on skills he or she excels in. Embrace shortcomings by acknowledging the weakness. Ask the Lord to give you the power to work out your issues so that your weaknesses do not manage you.

From a Trifling Act to a Treasured Response: Deuteronomy 30:19-20

Choose Life for goodness sake. Make a choice to live life; to hold fast to God's plan and purpose. When a woman observes over time that her man is directed by God, her ability to comply with his requests appears to step in time like the tango. It is time to move your relationship into alignment with God's directives instead of your own.

Knowledge + Understanding + Faith = Wisdom to use God's Word for His glory.

1. What decisions have you made which will improve your relationship with your spouse?
2. What double standards require attention?
3. The Lord says if you will follow His commands you will live and multiply. In what areas (physical, financial and social) is your prosperity being hindered because you are out of order according to God's Word?
4. How often are you studying the word of God and asking for revelation and understanding of His word?

Trifling Act Scene 3:
That's just the way I am

We have all heard people use the following statements to justify their inappropriate behavior. The statements are made to invoke the listener to accept the behavior as acceptable.

- "I am who I am and that is the way it is."
- "You knew I was this way when you married me."
- "If you don't like it, that is your issue not mine."
- "You have the wrong perception."

Please! It is time for you to stop covering your mess with excuses that slam against the wall and bounce back at the offender. None of the statements above are attractive or godly. Here is the deal. Just because you do not want to change your bad attitude or a poor habit does not mean people have to accept your mess. Let's use Darryl and I as an example of our gross misuse of "That's just the way I am."

I was accustomed to sleeping in my own bed and using all the covers, etc. But boy was I in for a rude awakening during our first month as a married couple. Darryl snored loudly and hogged the covers every night. After a week of fighting for the blanket and nudging him in the side to turn over, I had had it.

"Darryl! I can't sleep with you snoring in my ear all night. I need sleep just like you do!" Darryl said,

"Honey, I am so sorry, I did not realize my snoring was keeping you awake. Just nudge me and I will turn over. Also, we can look at getting a bigger bed." He seemed so sincere about changing that I felt badly about raising my voice to be heard. Let me tell you, after nudging Darryl for three weeks, sleep deprivation set in and the following words came out of his mouth. "Woman, I have been snoring all my life. You need to get used to it!" Of course that night someone had to sleep on the couch. I was hurt and dismayed that he would speak to his new bride in such a manner.

After a few days of the cold shoulder he relented and apologized for his outburst. He admitted that he probably should go to see a doctor about his snoring. We are an excellent example of how God gives you wisdom in spite of yourself. It also says a great deal about loving your spouse for who he or she is at the present time. This includes those habits that are not so attractive.

The Lord brought your spouse into your life in order to bring out the unique characteristics that are hidden deep inside of you. That is why we are attracted to people that are opposite to us. God wants us to be an original, an authentic representation of God's gift to the world. However, all of us are a work in process and we progress into becoming better each day. This means taking a good hard look at yourself and accepting your positive areas and those that require adjustments.

There is nothing attractive about an individual who states, "That's just the way I am" in an effort to justify rudeness, disobedience or disrespect. It demonstrates that you would rather stay stuck in a behavior which says "too bad, too sad". These types of behaviors say that the individual refuses to grow, learn, and seek

God's face in order to change. It reeks of the fear of change and insecurity.

Am I out of line?

Tina knew Jason used to go with his friends to strip clubs. She figured once they were married that "guy action" would stop. Jason didn't think there was anything wrong with hanging out with the guys as long as he got home in time for dinner and went to church on Sunday.

Tina: I need to talk to you now! We have a virus on our computer. It appears someone has been pulling up pornography links on our system.

Jason: Oh honey, it is just entertainment and there is no harm in it.

Tina: You have to be kidding me right? That is just like committing adultery and it is addictive.

Jason: You are over-reacting. My dad had playboy magazines around the house all the time. It is no big deal.

Tina: I can never stack up to those magazine women! You know that I do not feel comfortable with your habit.

Jason: Look, I need something to relax. You are always nagging me. I am a grown man. I don't have a problem. You are the one with the problem.

Tina: You need to get help before this "internet thing" ruins our relationship!

The challenge: Tina is confronted with standing in the gap for Jason while he works out his issues with pornography. Tina's mind is reeling to figure out where she went wrong with Jason. She thought her marriage would be perfect. Now more than ever, Tina must believe that God will give her the strength to hold fast. She must believe that God is in the middle of her situation. It would also help for Tina to find out from a professional, all she can about addictive behaviors. For Jason, he must admit that he has a problem before he will be willing to work out his issues.

What do you do when your husband or wife won't do right? What move do you make to address the problem? When your spouse demonstrates actions that are negative in nature and deliberately unhealthy, a conversion must happen from the inside out.

Only God can truly change the heart of a man or woman. Self evaluation is a critical part of the change process however. When was the last time you took a critical look at yourself? When was the last time you laughed loudly by yourself? If you cannot be happy with yourself how do you expect your spouse to receive your trifling self? The sincere, genuine observations of friends and family can be a wonderful start to making changes in your life.

Asking God how your current behavior lines up with His purpose, plan and Word is mandatory in order to progress into your divine purpose. The trouble with refusing to change is that it will result in people tolerating you instead of accepting you. It is more important to be accepted than tolerated. This requires balance and knowing the unique individual within you. Without balance your efforts can be perverted by others who see your efforts to change as a way to manipulate their will on you.

Ask yourself these questions:

1. If something were to happen to you today how would others remember you?
2. Will friends and family remember a loving spirit or a hateful spirit?
3. Do you demonstrate the right priorities in your life? (God, spouse, family, church - in that order.)
4. Do you accept your weaknesses and build on your strengths in order to be a witness to others?
5. Did you love hard, play hard and work responsibly?

Ladies and gentlemen now is the hour to know yourself and the positive impact you have on your spouse and those around you. God has given you an audience of one that looks lovingly into your eyes each day. Your spouse is seeking your love and acceptance. This requires taking hold of this great task and learning to be the best that God has called you to be. Do not continue to waste valuable time stuck in the same miserable place for the next 10-20 years.

From a Trifling Act to a Treasured Response: 1 Philippians 1:6

God is faithful to do what He said he will do. He is the God who swears by Himself that heaven and earth will pass away before His Word fails. Knowing God's Word won't fail gives you confidence. Your strength is built on Jesus Christ your intercessor. Actions that do not conform to God require revelation and repentance. Your perception is just that - yours. It does not make it right or appropriate, just your own mess. When you tell your spouse his/her viewpoint is wrong, you fail to grasp that you do not have the authority to change that viewpoint. However, you can provide your mate with more information, with which to challenge his/her thought process. Yet, even with extending additional information, it is up to the individual to change his/her view of you.

Ask yourself the following questions:

1. Are there areas in your life that require more information in order to improve how you view a situation or perceive a problem?

2. Are you trying to force a change on your spouse instead of laying your burdens at God's feet for Him to handle?

Trifling Act Scene 4: Are you a test dummy?

I really enjoy watching the crash tests (rigorous simulations of impacts) that car companies conduct to determine how effective an automobile handles under pressure. They remind me of the collisions we have with our spouses. In the test, an automobile races head on towards a brick wall. The objective is to see where the stress factors appear and how well the frame of the vehicle will protect the driver. The test dummy gets into the car each time, knowing that it is about to run headfirst into the wall. The test dummy has no other choice but to go with the program.

However, we do have options. How many times do we run ourselves into a wall when dealing with our spouses? How many times do we run head first into the same conflict and expect not to hit a brick wall? At some point we have to tell ourselves, I'm tired of being the test dummy and move out of the way of the oncoming brick wall! You know you can see the conflict coming directly towards you. The ability or inability to move or change direction comes from something within. Does your inability consist of fear, habit or a hardened heart?

The mind is a terrible thing to waste.

When the wife comes in from a long day at work, the husband wants to know what's for dinner. Now he has been sitting at home for the past two hours relaxing from his hard day at work. The wife has the option of running into the brick wall of listening to "a straight crazy husband" or she can turn the tables on this situation. "Honey, why don't we order pizza tonight, I've had a hard day." Collision averted on this model family today.

Unfortunately, hubby decides to test just how much pressure his wife can withstand. He is tired of pizza and complains that she is not performing her wifely duties lately. Now the wall is colliding with you. These are the times in which you can demonstrate what kind of faith you have. Scriptures say that what is in you will come out. This is why it is important to have a regular dose of the Word, including a regular prayer life.

Reading your Word stores the promises and presence of God within you. When the Word is absent in your life, you begin to trust in the world to feed you. Under pressure, what you have been feeding yourself spiritually; what you have spoken daily into your soul will come out. You will either respond from a position of faith or a position of self preservation (according to the world).

This wife has had a hard day dealing with rude employees and an unappreciative manager, now she comes home to an ungrateful husband? That's IT! The gloves come off and the discussion/fight begins.

Dialogue goes like this:

Wife: "Well if you made enough money, I would not have to work. I could sit at home cooking and cleaning just for you. I would meet you at the door with nothing but a see-through night gown."

Husband: "You are the one who wanted to buy this house. I was satisfied in the last house. It costs money to go on those vacations that we can't afford."

Why must we move to a position of inflicting hurt instead of moving to a position of understanding where the real issue emanates? God gave us the ability to make our own decisions. Scripture challenges us to choose life or death. Then the Lord gives you the answer, choose life.

Test dummies do not have enough sense to come out of the rain, let alone make decisions that are selfless, and show compassion. For each test, the test dummy must be taken out of the car to determine the damage done. If we could see just how damaging our words are toward others, our approach would be prayerfully, significantly different.

Guess what, in the end everyone in the house needs to eat unless you just decided that today will be a day of fasting and prayer. Finally, a test dummy does not have a brain. However, God gave us a brain and a free will that we can use to impact our environment. Use your head for more than a hat rack! Don't be a test dummy.

Darryl and I do our best to provide encouragement to couples as they work out their problems. We are honest and tell them what they need to know, not what they want to hear, to feel good. We use our experiences to help others avoid some of the same crazy things we have endured throughout our married life. Unfortunately, we have learned the reality that some folks can only learn a lesson by living the mistake and then wailing with God through the consequence.

Next to accepting Jesus Christ as your Lord and Savior, connecting with the one you love spiritually and physically is liberating and empowering. The Bible says to walk in a manner worthy of your calling. That calling begins as a witness of the love of Jesus. That calling should start with your own home first! Here is the deal, if your witness is not effective at home, then your witness outside of the home will be fake and without the full power of God's anointing. God has given you everything you need to minister to your spouse. He is giving you an opportunity to be an earthly witness of a mighty God.

A test dummy cannot attest to anything. God's children can attest to the goodness, the grace and the mercy of a heavenly Father. A test dummy will keep hitting the same wall expecting a different response. God has given you a mind and a spouse who will challenge your thought-process. Use them both to grow up in your faith. A test dummy is placed into a situation. You have the option of walking away from situations that will only result in a problem. *2 Thessalonians 5:22*, states that we should turn away from the appearance of evil. God has given you the ability to avoid events where you will be drawn into temptation. Just say no to things you cannot handle. This is why it is so important to ask God to give you an understanding of what you can handle. Seek out sound counsel that supports healthy communication and reconciliation with your spouse. Ask God to place your relationship in an environment that has a spirit of forgiveness and accountability.

From a Trifling Act to a Treasured Response: Mark 4:39

Fill your heart and mind with the transforming Word of God. The Word will calm your spirit and ease your soul. Once your body, soul and spirit reach a place of rest, God has an opportunity to use you for His purpose.

Have you put the Word of God on your situation, on your attitudes and on your marriage? Jesus woke up, rebuked the wind and said to the sea, Peace! Be still. The amazing power of the Lord can rebuke the storms in your relationship and cause the confusion to be still.

Ask yourself the following questions:

1. What are you declaring in your marriage?
2. Are you speaking Peace into your circumstances or trying to take care of things in your own power? Shouting, screaming and nagging will not produce long lasting results.
3. Are you allowing the world to determine how your witness should be demonstrated?

Trifling Act Scene 5:
Remember not to toot too loudly

When was the last time you spoke to someone who was so sure of themselves that you could not get a word in edgewise? How about when you were trying to warn a close friend that the relationship she is in should have stopped at the first date? Some people you cannot tell them anything. They are a legend in their own minds. Remember the rich man who built barns? He did not feel that they were big enough, so he tore them down and built bigger ones. (*Luke 12:18*) After he rebuilt the barns, the Lord took his life. Overconfidence can get an individual into a lot of trouble. Overconfidence will cause you to think only of yourself and your knowledge base instead of exploring all of the angles before making a decision. It is a condition I call "the sickness of self."

The sickness of self will cause you to demand authority in your home instead of learning how to give sound counsel. The sickness of self will close your ears, mind, and heart to the truth about yourself from those who know you best. The sickness of self will cause you to give advice, testify, and quote scripture regarding how to treat your family, only to have your family call you a hypocrite. You're a liar and the truth is not in you. These are the symptoms of living with the sickness of self. You wonder why God is not listening to your

27

complaints and disappointments. Maybe, just maybe, God is silent in order for you to hear just how loud your clanging symbol is resounding. "If I speak the languages of men and of angels, but do not have love, I am a resounding gong or a **clanging** cymbal." (*1 Corinthians 13:1*).

Believe it or not, people are listening and watching you to see if this whole relationship with God and your spouse really works. The devil has you "smelling yourself" and believing the hype of your own autobiography so that you cannot see ineffective and unproductive behavior. What ever happened to walking in a spirit of meekness? My husband is an excellent example of walking in meekness.

Darryl grew up as the oldest of three children and at that time was the largest kid in his class. He spent a great deal of time restraining himself because he was a "big guy". Kids began to pick on him because they knew he would not do anything. WRONG! Darryl did have a threshold. He would explode and kick someone's behind. Unfortunately, his schoolmates took his meekness as weakness.

When Darryl and I married, I felt that Darryl allowed people to use and abuse him. I would speak up before he would. He was just a little too calm for me; thank you very much. Yet Darryl's ability to be level-headed under pressure protected our family on many occasions.

The sickness of self will cause you to confuse an individual's ability to maintain self-control with your ability to dominate and manipulate a situation.

The sickness of self encourages disrespect for others and their level of expertise. The sickness of self blocks your blessings and vision.

The sickness of self will have you tooting your horn so loud that no one wants to stay around to hear what you have to say.

Thinking too highly of yourself

Emily: I told you not to pay the landscaper until he completed the job. Now this guy has left with all of our money.

Tim: How many times do you have to remind me that I failed you again? Stop trying to punk me!

Emily: I just want to point out that my father told you the guy was no go good. Now we have to borrow money to get the work done.

Tim: You know when you lost your wallet and we had to cancel all your credit cards, I didn't stress you about it. Even though we had to open new checking accounts, etc. in order to pay our bills. Why must you be so critical? I don't need another mother!

Emily: I am not your mother. My issue is that you have not moved to do anything about this problem. You know how you like to avoid taking responsibility for stuff.

Tim: For your information, I contacted the Better Business Bureau. Additionally, I contacted the credit card company and they have provided us with a provisional credit. If you would give me a chance, I can make a move without you. Why can't you give me the benefit of the doubt?

It is apparent from this conversation that Tim has made some questionable decisions in the past and

Emily is holding him to those previous mistakes. Emily will need to decide whether she will step out on faith and believe or will she hold Tim to his past? Additionally, Tim will need to continue to walk with God as he reaps the consequences of the poor decisions he has sown into his marriage.

From a Trifling Act to a Treasured Response: James 1: 14-16

The devil is calling Jesus to set the record straight. "Hey Jesus, says Satan. I just want to let you know that I had nothing to do with that brother or sister sinning. They were drawn away by their own lust. I just helped them out!" The devil is a thief and a liar. He lurks around waiting to jump at your weaknesses in order to draw you away from the will of God. You must be willing to root out the evil desires that reside within you, confess them to God and turn from the pure appearance of evil. Do not allow the enemy to block your ability to show love and kindness through words of affirmation.

Ask yourself the following questions:

1. Where have you lost sight of the many blessings your spouse provides on a regular basis?
2. Do you provide words of encouragement and support on a regular basis?
3. In what areas do you compete with your spouse instead of complementing each other?

4. Do you equate the headship of your house with your husband's paycheck?
5. Do you value the responsibility associated with maintaining a household?

Trifling Act Scene 6:
What do you mean, you didn't know?

Every year, on the second week in May, Jonathan goes on a hunting trip. Every year Jamie picks a fight with Jonathan two days before it is time for him to leave. Jonathan has learned this painful pattern. He will make a concerted effort several weeks prior to his departure to spend special undivided attention with his lovely wife to let her know that she is the most important person in his life. Not good enough. Jamie still gets bent out of shape, which causes a big blow up and causes Jonathan to be miserable the entire hunting trip.

Did she get it?

Jonathan: Honey, don't forget this is the week I leave for my hunting trip with the guys.

Jamie: Is this the week that it happens? I have so many things to do that I need your help with!"

Jonathan: I go on this trip the same month every year, how can you forget this is the week that I leave?"

Let the argument begin! Jonathan has not discovered that in order for Jamie to feel satisfied in

33

her flesh, she must have a big emotional breakdown with him to keep from thinking about her husband while he is gone for a week. The bottomline is that Jamie does not want Jonathan to go hunting anymore. Do you want to know why? Believe it or not it is not because she does not trust Jonathan to be gone for a week with a bunch of guys. Actually, Jamie does not trust herself to be without Jonathan for a week. Do you want to know why she is afraid to be alone?

Three years ago Jamie had an affair while Jonathan was on his hunting trip. She wanted to get back at Jonathan for leaving her every year. However, the short lived "tango" did not produce the satisfaction she expected. Since that time, her guilt or stronghold emotions are transferred to her husband. Strongholds tie you to the problem instead of releasing your spirit through the grace of God. Jamie's stronghold binds her mind to all types of wrong thinking. If she could have an affair, of course her husband could also be predisposed to have an affair while he is on his hunting trip.

In an effort to free herself from the chains of guilt and condemnation, Jamie confessed her sin to God and her pastor, but never addressed the issue with her husband. The consequence of hiding the truth from her husband has Jamie all tied up in knots, and suspicious of all Jonathan's activities.

We are really good about transferring our strongholds to others. Jamie is trying to hold Jonathan to the same level of guilt she continues to experience. Now Jonathan is questioning why his annual hunting trip is provoking an issue? The question that is just as deep is why doesn't Jonathan know there is a problem with his wife?

Do you want to know why Jonathan does not get it? Is it because Jonathan only attempted to pay special attention to Jamie a few weeks before his hunting trip is scheduled, each and every year, like clock work? Granted, Jamie did not happen to fall into someone else's arms. When a woman decides she is going to have sex, it is a calculated event. She was indeed looking for love in all the wrong places. Jamie is a faithful church going individual. Their family contributes to the church on a regular basis, with time and finances. Yet, they struggle trying to identify what really matters to each of them. Jonathan believes that bringing his paycheck home and not cheating on his wife is all that is required as a husband. He did not take an active role in finding out what mattered to Jamie. Granted, his pastor has spoken on several occasions about how important it is for husbands to treat their wives like Christ treats the church. That is how Jonathan got the bright idea to back up about four weeks before his hunting trip and take Jamie out to lunch, to dinner, and shopping. Yet, he never had the real spirit of giving Jamie what she really needed on a regular basis--- his undivided attention and affection.

Making the Word of God real in your life must include the spirit of the Word as well as the law of the Word. Jonathan did not have the spirit of the Word as it relates to honoring his wife as the precious jewel God gifted him with. With only the law of the Word working in your marriage, communication disconnects will continue to exist.

- What do you mean we are going to have a fight over this same thing again?

- What do you mean you didn't know that she feels lonely and unappreciated?
- What do you mean you didn't know that he wanted to feel respected in front of your friends instead of like a paycheck with legs?
- What do you mean you didn't know that you get more excited about a trip with a bunch of guys that are not saved than you do when you go out to dinner with her?
- What do you mean you don't understand how your marriage has reached the point of no return and divorce appears to be the only option available to "make" you happy?

Regardless of how you fail, God is still the heart fixer and the mind regulator. Admit your faults and move in the direction of healing and deliverance. Take your eyes off the person and look to God for your strength. If you were to take an even closer look at the environment, there is plenty of blame to go around in this relationship. The devil will feed you a pack of lies. The snake is excellent at twisting the truth. Whereas God's Word stands all by itself. The devil's goal is to get you focused on the person instead of the problem. God's Word is the only thing that can stand without dispute regarding the deceitful ways of the enemy.

When you try to take care of your spouse on your own, the results are temporary and incomplete. However, your behavior towards your spouse becomes a testimony of how the power of God changes your situation. The Word is what convicts and challenges the heart of a Christian. Conviction leads you to conversion, which leads you to freedom. Freedom to love your spouse the way you really should. Freedom to demonstrate mercy and grace, where previously you told yourself if that ever happened in your relationship, you would terminate the relationship.

Secret sins are the best weapons that the devil uses to cause separation and division in relationships. As difficult as it may be to confess and deal with the consequences of your actions, it is far better to admit and quit than to be bound and condemned. We all have sinned and come short of the glory of God. (*Romans 3:23*) Yet, Jesus said "Forgive them Lord, they know not what they do."

From a Trifling Act to a Treasured Response: Hebrews 13:4-6

Marriage must be respected by all! That means even by the folks who know you are married and still attempt to chase you around the office building to get your phone number. Infidelity is damaging to the marriage bed. Your mind should be concentrating on one person not multiple possibilities! Declare a confession of faith over your marriage. Confess your sins to God and receive His Grace which is more than sufficient to see you through your storm. Know that God will never leave or forsake you.

In evaluating these scriptures, you will find that first Paul speaks of respecting the marriage bed, then moves to money, and ends with being satisfied with what we have. Being satisfied does not mean staying complacent with your current situation. Fight for every promise God has placed in your life. If your sex life is not what you want it to be, work with your spouse to make it happen for you both.

Consider the following:

1. Where does your attitude require adjustments toward respecting and honoring your love life?

2. What have you taken for granted regarding feeding your spouse physically and emotionally?

3. Intimacy and Sex are two different things. Have you determined the difference between the two actions? Where do you need to change your schedule to meet the needs of your spouse?

Trifling Act Scene 7: Selective Ignorance

Birthday, Valentine's Day, and Christmas happen every year at the same time, yet you still forget to honor your spouse in a special way.

What in the world is that all about?

Selective ignorance means you have decided to pick and choose when you have knowledge of something. It somehow allows you to play "dumb", which takes you off the hook of being responsible. Wrong, Wrong, and Wrong again.

- You know good and well that Valentine's Day is in February. Yet, you have to attend a business dinner on the 14th. Adding insult to injury, you forget to make any arrangements before the 14th to show you care to give the very best....because you forgot.
- His 40th birthday has come and gone without a word from you...because you forgot.
- Your wedding anniversary is the same month every year, but you forgot to do anything.
- All the guys were going to the annual golfing tournament, but you forgot and scheduled an early birthday party for your son. Then you make him feel guilty for not attending a family function.
-

- You remember every basketball statistic known to man, but you can't remember to pay the bills on time.....because you forgot.
- Your husband works at night, but you get up early in the morning and turn all the lights on so that he can't sleep....because you forgot.
- This is the first anniversary of the death of your deceased mother-in-law and your spouse is struggling with the memory of the loss. Yet you make no attempt to reach out to him in an effort to show support and concern....because it appears you forgot.

All of these are examples of selective ignorance. These are opportunities which inflict pain and disappointment in areas that are the tenderest in nature to the one you sleep with every night. In your mind, your spouse is supposed to understand, right? Likewise, another painful part of selective ignorance is ignoring when your spouse is struggling with an issue and you show no compassion or concern for his or her pain. A marriage cannot continue to function under a shroud of ignorance. Educate yourself on the most important project of your life...your spouse.

Relationships require effort and time. Selective ignorance states you have selected to abdicate your responsibility and demonstrate to your spouse that he or she is not worthy of your time or energy. Additionally, many of us have perfected manipulative ways of placing guilt on your spouse in order to release your responsibility.

I am not saying that you are responsible for the happiness of your spouse. The reality is you cannot make anyone happy who does not want to be. Ask a teenager who refuses to receive consolation after being dumped by a boyfriend or girlfriend. However, you are responsible for your actions. Those actions must exemplify a level of concern and a desire to tend to the other's needs, over your own. That ugly "selfish" head seems to elevate itself higher than the needs of your spouse.

Your spouse is a valuable gift who requires time and attention. You should not have to pull something out of your intestinal tract in order to understand your spouse's yearning for attention; you need each other. Money, clothes, toys and credit cards cannot hug you at night, wipe tears from your eyes or pray for you in the midnight hour. Newsflash people! If you do not appreciate and respect the gift God has given, you may find yourself without any gift at all.

Over the thousands of couples we have counseled, we have identified three killers of a marriage. The three big killers of marriage are money, sex, and family.

- When a couple establishes a pattern of making a living instead of living life with one another, neglect has an opportunity to slip into the marriage.
- When you take for granted that your spouse will always be there for you regardless of how you treat them, neglect has an opportunity to slip into the marriage.
- When you spend more time taking care of other family members instead of your own

family, neglect has an opportunity to slip into the marriage.

Neglect will cut off the circulation in a marriage. Just like a pair of pantyhose that are too tight, neglect cuts off the circulation in your marriage. When you fail to water plants on a regular basis they die. Failing to water your marriage with love and support will cause premature death. Instead of selective ignorance, pray for purposeful revelation. Ask God to show you where your actions do not provide a positive example for your spouse, your children and others. Determine through prayer which relationships need to be cut off because they are not fruitful. Evaluate areas in your marriage that require repairing the exposed stress cracks of the foundation caused due to neglect. Strive to establish a home, which is conducive to an environment of love and support.

From a Trifling Act to a Treasured Response: 2 Corinthians 9:7

God loves a cheerful giver, so does your spouse! One of the greatest gifts you can give your spouse is the gift of time. Whether that is personal space time or time dedicated exclusively with you, time is a valuable gift to receive from a loved one. Sowing time and attention to your spouse will reap a harvest of understanding and appreciation. Additionally, when you chose to serve your spouse, to purchase gifts or celebrate with your time and attention, remind yourself that your reward lies in serving for the sake of serving. When you serve for the sake of serving, you will not expect anything in return from your mate. You serve because God has given you the gift of your spouse to be a demonstration of God's love personified in the flesh. God is clear on when you give to others, be sure your motives are loving, kind and obedient to His will.

1. How many ways can you provide gifts-monetary or non-monetary - to your spouse to show you care?
2. Have you established a family calendar that lists all significant events and occasions in your family's life?
3. What family traditions have you established to honor events or occasions in your life.

Trifling Act Scene 8:
Are you married or are you single?

J esus said let your yea be yea and your nay be nay. In other words, be sure you know where you stand. An individual's martial status should not be a guessing game. You should present yourself in a way that says, "Yeah, I'm married!" When an individual is straddling the fence about their marriage, you invite a compromising altercation. Your posture says everything about where your marriage stands. Who you associate with is another indication of how you value your relationship.

One example of questionable association is hanging out with the wrong crowd. You know your spouse doesn't care for a certain group of people you associate with, yet you continue to go to functions because you are invited. Another example of a potential conflict is those special single friends that you keep in close contact with, yet your spouse has never met them or talked to them socially.

Pick a side and stay on it. Do the people on your job know you have a wife for real, or did that picture come with the wallet when you bought it? These scenarios are examples of a lack of respect and consideration for your spouse. It also says that you lack respect for the covenant of marriage and the importance of what marriage represents to God.

45

Here is the acid test. You are attending a big corporate meeting. The CEO of the company spends 10 minutes with you to get to know you personally. Later the CEO invites everyone to dinner and includes bringing your spouse or significant other. After the meeting the CEO walks by you and states he hopes to see you there with a date. It is obvious your conversation about who you are did not include your spouse!

How you present yourself tells the average man or woman that you are not available and don't even think about walking this way with that foolishness. Even when you do present yourself as "taken" predators in this world still try to approach you when the opportunity presents itself.

Flirting is a dangerous activity to engage in when you have committed yourself to another. Men seem to be in a state of disbelief when it comes to another woman flirting with them. It is a head game for the man that another woman other than his wife would be attracted to him. Why in the world would a woman want another woman's husband makes as much sense as you walking in the middle of a busy street.

Flirting gives the world the impression that you are available...even when you are not! Those events which only you can attend, makes me wonder whether they know that you have a spouse who should be included in the invitation. I also wonder why you have not challenged the fact that your better half was not invited. Don't get me wrong, my husband attends corporate meetings without me on a regular basis. But believe you me, when Darryl walks out the door, he has my scent all over him. It is a scent that says, "I am a married man. I belong to a woman who loves me as much as I love her!" The scent is enhanced by the way Darryl presents himself to others.

Let me give you an example of how my scent is all over Darryl when he attends meetings or dinners without me. First of all, Darryl is quick to speak lovingly of me. Second, he references how we make decisions regarding events that matter to him in his conversations with others. Darryl exhibits a demeanor that says I love my wife. He walks in a way that says, "I have drawn a line in the sand, and I am a married man."

If you have a proclivity toward flirting, maybe you are one of those folks who function as a married/single couple. Oh you're married, but everything is handled from a singleness mentality. When it comes time to pay bills, you separate the bills out by his bills and her bills. She pays the electric and trash, and he's responsible for the mortgage payment.

Forget about the blessing of tithing because you are too busy trying to make sure you can pay your share of the bills. He has his own schedule, and she has her own schedule. They happen to meet up at the end of the day in the same room in the same bed. This is what I call a living arrangement not a marriage. I would say the sex is also safe. Yet, there is no telling if a marriage of this kind is exclusively monogamous. As society talks about men being on the "down low", it is a low down shame that folks can not figure out married behavior compared to single behavior.

When she runs out of money because of an unexpected bill, which was probably her Macy's card, he says it is not his problem. So then the electricity is turned off. Are you crazy? Why didn't you pay the electric bill? Now both of you are living in the dark! Wow, you really showed her now didn't you? Honestly, I have never understood this concept.

When a couple marries, the two become one: one household, one commitment and one obligation to meet each other's needs. The women's liberation movement was never meant to tear down the institution of marriage. Men, your spouse's portfolio is not an indication of whether she would make a good wife and mother. Women, your husband's earning potential is not a surety of financial freedom.

From a Trifling Act to a Treasured Response: 1 Peter 3:15

Your relationship is a light of the goodness of God. When you reverence the Lord over your own flesh, your behavior will exemplify the righteousness of God. People observe how you function and desperately want to know if this Jesus thing is real. This is not to say you must be a perfect witness, but a witness you are none the less. Start your demonstration of love at home! When a majority of your heart is set on pleasing God, doing His will, seeking His face in order to be a better witness, your witness toward your spouse will be in line. You will smile more, even when your spouse is acting crazy because your hope is in the fact God will deal with him or her. As you walk in the power of God working for you, the Word says God demands an accounting of where your hope comes from.

1. Do you check your vocabulary before you open your mouth?
2. Are there single tendencies that require adjusting? (Old single friends, bar hopping, etc.)
3. Do your actions represent those of a married person?
4. Have you laid hold of the hope God has placed in your marriage?

Trifling Act Scene 9: Go ahead and bad mouth your spouse!

Go ahead and bad mouth your spouse, you married him/her! Every morning during the first coffee break, Tim complains about what his wife is not doing for him. Jennifer, Tim's co-worker, chimes in to add complaints about her husband. Fred, a single man, has spent the past three months observing this dialogue. He finally speaks up and says, "Were your marriages arranged? Did someone make you marry your spouse?" Both Tim and Jennifer stated effectually, "Of course not". Fred then states something insightful, "Then who is the fool, if your relationship is not working out?" Fred walks out of the coffee room with Tim and Jennifer staring at himwith their mouths wide open. Amazing how those on the outside looking in, can be so insightful!

You are a reflection of your spouse, whether you like it or not. Don't get me wrong, we make our own decisions and we can only be responsible for our actions and not our spouse's reactions. In theory this makes sense. However, my actions do affect my spouse. I will respond to the environment in which I am exposed. So something in my home environment is contaminating my ability to manage according to your expectations. **Translation**: Find out what in the world is going on at home instead of complaining about it.

51

Additionally, be willing to ask questions and prepare yourself to accept the responses.

Can't we get along?

Jennifer comes home frustrated about her coffee conversation. In an off-cuff manner, Jennifer uses the conversation to verbalize her disappointment with her husband, Richard.

Jennifer: Why can't our marriage be like the Jones'? We never go anywhere or do anything.

Richard: Honey, I would love to go out to dinner with you. However, we decided when we purchased this house that the first year would be tight for the family.

Jennifer: It is always about money. You just do not meet my needs anymore.

Richard: Why would you say that? You wanted a bigger house. I worked two jobs to come up with the down payment. Now we are in the house and you are still not satisfied. I can't do enough for you. Your mind changes like the wind! What do you want from me, woman?

It appears that the other shoe has dropped on this conversation. Anytime there is a failure to communicate in a relationship, both individuals must take responsibility. You say, "How can that be? If my spouse does not talk to me that should not be my fault." Communication is a two-way street. There is a sender and a receiver in every conversation. It is the sender's responsibility to articulate the message in a way or manner the receiver can understand. For

52

example: If Darryl is in the middle of the street and I am whispering "Get out of the middle of the road", he will not hear nor can he respond. If I want to avert an accident, I need to alert Darryl to the impending danger. The automobile is about to hit him and he needs to get out of the street.

Likewise if the receiver perceives that the sender is trying to communicate, the receiver has an obligation to respond in a way that states the message was delivered effectively....or not. If Darryl turns and sees me acting crazy, even if he can't hear me, he knows I have a concern.

What is not effective is devaluing your spouse in order to justify the effort needed to find an effective way to reach your audience. At some point in time you may have heard someone devalue their mate.

Was that really necessary?

"That was a stupid remark." Anthony states to Michelle. This comment was in response to Michelle's opinion regarding a recent movie they had seen. This comment was also made in front of another couple. The other couple tried to lighten the atmosphere by stating, "Oh, it is no big deal. We really liked the movie." Anthony then proceeds to go a little further with his public insults. "She is always talking about something without knowing all the information." Michelle reverts to a silent position for the rest of the dinner. Later at home, Anthony wonders why Michelle is cold and distant. It is because he was trifling!

You can't bad mouth your spouse in public and become confused about the consequences. There is a consequence to devaluing your spouse. You devalue your relationship and yourself. Is it possible that the couple never learned enough about each other before they became one? Is it possible that the husband did not know the value of lifting up his spouse in her low places? Is it possible that the wife did not appreciate all the hard work her husband did in order to please his wife? Is it possible that you know just how damaging your words are and feel this behavior is necessary to cause a change? Pain and envy are dangerous partners. These negative emotions cloud your vision and the real issue.

Ask yourself this question, what did I see in my mate in the first place? When you can remind yourself what attracted you to your spouse in the first place, you will move your spirit to a position of thanksgiving and praise for your mate. This move of God in your heart will challenge you to check your thought-processes and actions before expecting your spouse to make any changes. Instead of complaining about what is wrong in the relationship, focus on those things that are good, pleasant and of good report. Our society has a habit of psychoanalyzing everything to the point of depression and wondering how we got into this mess in the first place.

Did you ever consider that maybe you are the first person who requires mending instead of your spouse? Only God can change the heart of man. Marriage is not something that just happens. A great marriage is developed and nourished every day in order for you to see real progress over the life of the marriage. It is easier to complain than to move in a direction of positive change.

Life and death are in the power of the tongue. Your tongue is a weapon that is unleashed on a regular basis. Here is another example of an unbridled statement: "Anyone with a brain knows that you cannot do that." **Translation**: Anyone with a brain (stupid) knows that you cannot do that (dummy)!

When you move in a direction where you want to be understood and seek to understand, your conversations change. "Help me understand why you believe that way?" "I really do not agree with that decision, but I do trust that you know how we should move".

Yet, is it possible that there is another reason why you fail to have self control. Is it possible that you do not trust your spouse, and now you want to justify your dissatisfaction with your decision to marry him/her by complaining out loud to the point of embarrassing him/her publicly? In the words of Aretha Franklin, "Who's zooming who?" His mistakes are your mistakes - you are one. If nothing else, learn to trust God each day. The scripture says that through God's Spirit and your faith that all things work together for the good for those who love the Lord. (*Romans 8:28*) Put your faith into the pain of disappointment you feel and rest in believing that God will work it all out for your good and God's glory. Make a decision to speak life each and every day instead of death.

From a Trifling Act to a Treasured response: Philippians 4: 8

Think on those things that are honorable and just and pure and lovely. When was the last time you admired your spouse as an individual of beauty made by God? Spend an entire week looking for the good in your spouse. Pursue peace instead of confrontation. Imagine just how peaceful your relationship and household would be if you do.

1. Make a list of examples where you pursue peace in your relationship?
2. Are your words a source of strength or a tool for destruction?

Trifling Act Scene 10:
Use your head for more than a hat rack.

My grandmother is a wonderfully wise and down to earth woman of God. When you would do something crazy, she would say "Girl, use your head for more than a hat rack!" Use the brain God gave you to articulate what you believe, not just to hold your hat on straight. Your head should be used to do more than hold a hair style. The thought in itself should cause us to laugh and then ponder what this statement really infers. When you have a problem with your relationship, who do you go to? When the Lord has convicted your behavior and your soul struggles to repent and then apologize where do you seek counsel?

Today's society will go logical before going spiritual. You will allow people ill-equipped in marital issues to counsel you regarding your spouse. You will use the world's understanding about how to honor and respect your spouse before going to the book of the Bible which commands husbands to love your wives, and wives to submit to their own husbands. The problem with the world's view of marriage is that it has no strength. The moment you have an issue in your marriage there is no covenant to seek God's counsel instead of taking matters into your own hands.

What were you thinking?

Jason just found out that his girlfriend is pregnant. Problem, big problem, why? Jason is married with children. Jason's chest tightens as Suzie speaks softly into the phone advising him that he is going to be a father. Additionally, she feels that this is a great opportunity for Jason to leave his wife of 15 years. After all, he could not possibly be in love with his wife because he was having an affair with her.

Jason: I am not leaving my wife, and how do I know this child is mine? I have not seen you in months.

Suzie: Well it has been exactly 2 months since we slept together. I am 6 weeks pregnant. You are the father.

Jason calls David, his best friend from the Men's Ministry at the church. David and Jason decide it is in Jason's best interest to cover up the truth. Additionally, Jason will leave it up to Suzie to decide if she will keep the baby. This way it is not his problem that Suzie decided to keep the baby. Suzie is now devastated. She just knew if she got pregnant that Jason would do the responsible thing and leave his wife. That was her plan all along. Oh, by the way, I forgot to tell you that Suzie is the choir director at her church. Jason is a trustee at the same church. Now the shoe has just dropped. Of course it appears to everyone that Mary, Jason's wife, does not know these two have been going at it like rabbits for the past six months. Jason has failed to use his head for more than a hat rack. God is not going to bless your mess. Repent and ask God for direction and guidance. God will give you the strength to get you through whatever consequence that results from the seed you have sown, and walk with you through the winters of your life.

What goes on in the dark will come to the light. Suzie has an idea; she will contact Mary. Now the party begins. Yet something unexpected happens. Mary is not hysterical or ranting and raving about how disappointed she is in her husband. There is a haunting silence on the other end of the phone.

Mary has known for some time that her husband was cheating on her. As a matter of fact, she spoke with her Elder regarding the issue several months prior. The Elder stated that she was overreacting and that she had a good man. Unless she had physical proof with photos, the Elder refused to respond to her suspicions. It is really unclear how the church should have responded to Mary's concerns. Infidelity and abuse continue to haunt the body of Christ. Leaders are either afraid or oblivious of the situation. Silence is a form of agreement. As a result, individuals presume that they are safe to continue in their disobedience because no accountability has been required. Let's get back to the rest of the story.

The reason Mary is calm is because Jason had a little talk with Jesus and told Him all about his troubles. He confessed his sins to Mary about a week ago. She accepted his confession of infidelity. Now the mending must begin.

It is all over but the crying!

Mary: I have been waiting for your call Suzie.

Suzie: I am carrying your husband's baby. I wanted you to know.

Mary: You wanted me to know to see what I was going to do, right?

Suzie: Yes, he needs to take responsibility for his actions?

Mary: Have you taken responsibility for your actions? You knew that Jason was married. Yet, you chased after him anyway... I would also speculate that you planned to get pregnant as well. I told my husband that there were women out there like you and he did not believe me.

Suzie: That's a lie. Your husband loves me.

Jason: No Suzie, I do not love you.

Suzie is now silent on the phone. She had no idea that Jason was on the other line with his wife.

Mary: From now on, you will deal directly with me. If you need something for the baby, you will contact us both. No more secret conversations. Additionally, my husband has contacted Pastor Ray-Ray and advised him of the situation. You will probably get a call from him in the near future. Good day Suzie.

Using your head for more than a hat rack declares you will not allow the devil to convolute the situation any further. It means accepting whatever the consequences, are including stepping down from positions that influence the weak and the young. God will have your back and go before you to make your crooked road straight. God imparts grace to His children. In *Jeremiah 31:13*, God states he will turn your mourning into joy and provide gladness for sorrow.

Many times we want to take God's grace for granted and abuse His mercy that is renewed daily. At some point, God will say that's enough and take His hands off your situation in order for you to learn and grow. Seek the Lord while you can find Him.

From a Trifling Act to a Treasured Response: Matthew 18:20-22

First Jesus tells His disciples He would be in the middle of their situation if two or three are gathered together. Then He tells Peter – FORGIVE! Jesus knew the importance of standing united in order to bring the presence of God into your situation. Unforgiveness will hinder your ability to stand in agreement with each other. Invite Jesus to be in the midst of your marriage. Forgiving someone who has wronged you is not an easy task. Forgiving your spouse will release you from the bonds of strife. Forgiveness releases you from allowing an individual to rule over you. The offence continues to play like a bad movie in your head. Forgive and move on to a position of healing. Vengeance is mine, says the Lord. (*Deuteronomy 32:35*)

Start today by asking God to forgive you of your sins and then to release the offences that others had inflicted on you. Many folks that have hurt us continue on with their lives, while you live wounded. Decide to move out of the broken, disappointed places of your life and into the light of possibilities.

Trifling Act Scene 11:
The games people play

My son is an excellent chess player. His primary goal when competing with an opponent is to win. His focus is strategic and calculated. His goal is to win. Therefore, he will spend an extensive amount of time studying techniques to improve his success rate. It is his attempt to know his strengths and his weaknesses before his opponent discovers his problem areas.

When people play games, they play to win. To improve your game, you must know yourself and your opponent. Whether you are single or married, knowing who you are improves your ability to combat the devils in your life. When you know who you are and whose you are in Christ Jesus, the struggles of this world can be endured. Yet your encounters with others can place you in a position of compromise.

Many single folks do not understand the consequences of connecting with an individual physically or emotionally. Each encounter you terminate has the potential of leaving a part of you with them. This is why it is so important to build yourself up in your Holy places. God is everything you need. As you engage in relationships, use your discernment before emotionally committing yourself to someone. Look for Godly characteristics in an individual. There are too many people in the world who have a trifling mentality as it relates to dating and connecting with others. They think dating is a game. The game called life must equate to more than just winning. The world believes that in order for someone to win, someone has to lose. If you don't know who you are before you get into the game, you can be easily persuaded to behave outside of your character.

Let the games begin

Stephanie would call Jimmy every afternoon and get into an argument. She really wants to break off the relationship; however, she never learned how to release herself the right way from a relationship. So the only way she knows how to break off a relationship with a guy is to play the head game: call and hang up. Call again and then hang up on him. He calls, and she will not answer the phone. She calls and states she wants to date other people, and then realizes that she does not have anyone else to date. This cat and mouse game goes on until someone curses the other person out and the relationship is then ended. This type of behavior actually conditions the person into believing that this is the best way to end a relationship. It is seen as effective and becomes comfortable, even though to the other individual it is painful and ineffective. It leaves them broken, disconnected, and bitter.

Once you get tired of playing the head game, you finally release your life to God who directs you to a spouse. If you dated for any length of time, both of you may be very efficient at playing the "head game." Strongholds of this nature are hard to break without calling on God to help you out. Without the proper counseling, the way to your spouse's heart could be through manipulation. The lasting effects of unhealthy relationships then transfer into your marriage.

The drama continues: Two people who are not whole get married. Half a person and half a person do not make a whole person. It just makes two people who are broken candidates for healing and deliverance. Where are you wounded? Are your injuries deep? Can you recover without injuring your spouse in the process? You can actually make great music together if you can just transition into becoming one as God intended it to be.

People are in such a hurry "nowadays." They are in a hurry to make decisions that can impact them for the rest of their lives. Then they wonder why God has not brought them out. We are in a hurry to see revelation in our lives. "I want my spouse to act right now!" PLEASE, it took at least a good week for your husband to figure out it was not acceptable to cut his toe nails during dinner. You are in a rush to get engaged. You rush to get married. You rush to find a reason why the marriage is not working out. When all the dust settles, what was the real rush in the first place? Every good thing comes from God in His time and for His glory. God is a wonderful teacher if you have the patience to learn for the rest of your life. Transition is part of transformation. It takes time to allow the process to evolve.

It's time to make a change.

Take the example of Michelle and Jim. Michelle has had it up to her eyeballs with Jim and his track team. One of the special characteristics that Jim exhibits is his passion for children and building up their self esteem. He takes calls at any time of the day and night to speak words of encouragement to children who rarely get any type of positive reinforcement at home. On the outside these acts of selfless dedication appear to be admirable. The problem is, Jim did not establish boundaries and create a balance in his life. Therefore, Jim and Michelle have not had a vacation in four years. It is not because they cannot afford it. Jim does not feel anyone is competent to cover for him if he were to go on vacation. According to Michelle, she is always an afterthought to Jim. Jim defends his position by stating that the children need him and his wife should understand that he is making a sacrifice now for the future.

Is it my turn yet?

Michelle: What about our future? You hardly have time for your own children. I feel like a single parent. I may as well be divorced. Your own children signed up for track just to see you on a regular basis. Then you come home and you want us to run to you with opened arms. Your track team is more important than your own family.

Jim: That is not true. We have family day at least once a week. I am not cheating on you and I bring my paycheck home every two weeks. Woman, what else do you want from me?

Michelle: I want you to attempt to spend as much time with your family and me as you do with your track team.

Jim: You knew when you married me that I was an athletic coach. Why is it that now you do not approve? I thought "we" had an understanding.

Michelle storms off to the bedroom and locks the door.

Michelle married Jim because she was lonely and was tired of looking for the right man in the wrong places. Where else better to meet someone than at the gym? You get the privilege of observing a man to see if he flirts or if he concentrates on his workout. Jim married Michelle because he wanted someone who was physically attractive and who consistently maintained her figure. Both of them were broken in places where they were very effective in camouflaging their wounds. Jim is tired of defending his passion for what he does for a living, and Michelle is tired of being low on his priority list. Both need to identify priorities in their relationship.

From a Trifling Act to a Treasured Response: Ephesians 5:29-31

Where are your priorities? Do you have balance in your life? Does that balance include submitting to the plan God has established for you and your spouse? Jesus demonstrated His love for you by dying on the cross. He gave you an example of what is important.

When a man leaves his father and mother and clings to his wife as one flesh, the priority is to care for one another. The mystery of "the two will become one flesh" is that without God, two people with different backgrounds, educations and emotions combined cannot move as one whole force pounding with one heartbeat. As you walk as one unified front, decisions are made which meet the needs of the family.

Trifling Act Scene 12:
Are you under the influence?

Are there times when you get the impression that your spouse is smoking or drinking some type of mind altering drug that just made the street market? "How in the world could you not know that our finances would be impacted if you took $10,000 out of the savings account to give to Booboo the fool to invest? What were you thinking?" Let's try another twist on this under the influence concept. There is nothing like living life on a natural high....However, there is something else to be said about the other types of highs we get off on within our relationships. Let's take a look at a few examples of how we tend to enjoy observing our spouse fail.

- Your spouse insisted he needed that new $1200 gas grill. You tried to encourage him to get a professional to install the grill. Your husband said it was a piece of cake to hook the gas line up to the grill. After the fire department put out the flames, the grill is not worth a dime. You spend the rest of the year telling everyone the embarrassing news at the expense of your husband.

- You could hardly wait to tell your wife, "I told you so". She is bent on having a tan Gucci bag. Everyone who is anyone has a Gucci bag. Not that you are against your wife having nice things, but you resent the reason why your wife

69

wants the bag. The Gucci bag is stolen at the gym.

- Your husband told you not to go out to the night club with the girls. Staying out with single friends on a regular basis is not healthy. He continues to question

  why you have no married friends. At the club, you happen to run into one of the members from the church. This male Christian tries to make a move on you and you don't resist. You go home to tell your husband what happened because you enjoy getting your spouse upset over you.

When you are dealing with the emotions of others, your influence can and will have some type of significance. Your impact on your environment is predicated on how you behave, not on what you say. Whether you are feeding yourself negative enforcement or outside forces are encouraging non-productive behavior, you must learn who and what is influencing your marriage. We encourage couples to seek out other strong Christian couples who can lift them up and encourage their marriage. So when you get in a position that is unfamiliar, there is someone who can challenge your thought-process and with the Holy Spirit convict you and redirect your steps.

The devil's job is to distract and distort the truth. If you do not know who you are and whose you are, then the devil has done his job of putting your relationship off track.

And the Lord shall make thee the head, and not the tail; and thou shall be above only, and shall not be beneath; if that thou hearken unto the commandments of the Lord thy God, which I command thee this day, to observe and to do them (Deut 28:13). You are to behave in a manner that is of God. This is not to say that everything you do must be perfect. On the contrary, it means you are doing what you can to be obedient to God.

The Bible contains the blue print to lead us closer to His likeness. As the head, your husband must listen with compassion and understanding. Words of encouragement, speaking with integrity, and clarification of right intentions, are all areas that improve your ability to speak life instead of death into your relationship. Working to master these techniques require time, patience and longsuffering by both husband and wife. From the fall of Adam and Eve, men and women have struggled with exposing their imperfections. As stated before, Adam and Eve did not only hide themselves from God with their fig leaves, they also hid themselves from each other. Since the garden we have continued to hide things from each other.

Just say no!

Angela has developed the art of shopping. This art has caused the entire family to struggle financially because of her insistence on purchasing unnecessary items that are outside of the family budget. She has a really bad habit of purchasing items that she will wear a few times, wash a few times, and then get bored with the style. Angela has gone on shopping binges during her lunch hour and hid the shopping bags in her car trunk or even over at her girlfriend's house. Then she slowly moves them into her closet hoping that her husband will not notice the new dress or the new shoes. The situation has become so desperate that Anthony opened a separate checking account so that the daycare and mortgage payments would clear the bank. Anthony refuses to seek counseling for his wife and himself because he is embarrassed that the situation has gone too far and does not want his information advertised. Anthony has resorted to separating out the bills, hoping that this act will force Angela to take responsibility for her actions and change her behavior.

Anthony: Angela, I thought you said the electric bill was paid. We just received a cut off notice today!

Angela: I didn't have the money to pay the bill.

Anthony: What happened to the money? The bill is 3 months past due. Where are the other bills?

Angela: What I do with my money is my business. You said that I do not need to know what you're doing with your money, so I don't need to tell you what I am doing with mine.

Anthony: So if all of us are sitting in the dark is that fine with you? What kind of example are you making for our children and for those so called friends of yours? I am tired of working overtime to make ends meet.

To say the least the conversation continues without resolution. The marriage is out of order. The couple is not functioning with one goal and one purpose. God is a God of order and peace. This family could definitely use an "Out of Order" sign to hang on their door. Angela is under the influence of self and immediate gratification. Her conscience does not appear to be concerned for her family. Angela is out of order in her family. She has taken on an attitude that does not honor or respect her husband or her family. She has forgotten that her choices are producing problems for her family. Obviously a change must take place to put this family back on track.

From a Trifling Act to a Treasured Response: James 4:6, 7

God gives grace to the humble. Humble yourself before God. Take God at His Word and ask for strength while you walk through this season in your life.

Step one: Submit to God.
Step two: Resist the devil.
The result: Evil flees. Give it up for King Jesus!

Imagine if you have a magical mirror, which revealed every flaw that existed within.
1. Would the mirror expose a prideful heart?
2. Would the mirror show concern for self or concern for others?
3. Would the mirror uncover some deep dark secret that you have not resolved?

Trifling Act Scene 13: Hot Water or Hot Grits – they both burn

The problem with hot water and hot grits is that both burn extensively leaving scars that are difficult to heal. Much like the scars of physical abuse and verbal abuse, these scars are carried for years within an individual. When you elect to take out physical aggression on your spouse, you have stepped out of line of what God commanded marriage to be. God says do not touch His anointed. Many believe this verse only refers to ministers. Yet, we all minister to one another. God will not allow your abuse to go unnoticed or without judgment.

Abuse is abuse

Tina and Ethan have been married for over 18 years. Their marriage has been on the edge for years. Tina told herself that next time it would be different. She would fight back. It was not right for Ethan to verbally and physically abuse her. The last straw occurred when she went to the church for help and the minister told her if she would only cook and clean more often, then Ethan the Elder would not be provoked. Additionally, the minister assured her that he would speak to Ethan privately because this was a man's reputation at stake.

Tina is ashamed and dismayed. Reflecting on her marriage, Tina realized that Ethan had a proclivity for being abusive before they were married. However she thought that after they were married it would stop. She remembers "windows of time" during their 8 month engagement period when Ethan would chastise Tina about what she was wearing to church or how she wore her hair. In retrospect, she can recall four occasions where Ethan caused bruises on her arms from twisting them too hard. Yet Tina's desire to have a "Godly man", with status in the church, outweighed her discernment. She just knew that her influence on Ethan could soften his heart.

The problem is Tina does not have the power to change the heart of man, only God does. She can be a strong influence, and a strong model of love to her husband, but she cannot change him. Ethan's issues with abuse required more expertise than Tina possessed. The best and first thing Tina can do for Ethan is encourage and pray for him. Unfortunately, the physical abuse became worse when Ethan found out from the minister that his wife had sought counsel with the church. Ethan refused to believe that his behavior was inappropriate. After all, he is the head of the house. If Tina would just do what he told her, then things would be fine. As probably expected, Tina leaves the home after a recent altercation with Ethan's fist to her right eye. She returns to the church to show them proof and left the church never to return again. The reality is spousal abuse happens in the church. It is a problem that requires exposure and support instead of denial and resistance.

Is this trifling? Of course it is! One must decide to take responsibility and take action. Regardless of how difficult it may be, empower yourself and walk away from the abusive relationship. Do not allow anyone to determine your selfworth. Resorting to throwing hot water or hot grits is not the answer. You may feel good for a little while, but it is not the answer. This is not to say you are giving up on your marriage. However, you may need to have an intervention to mend the relationship. What if you could turn back the hands of time with this couple? How could this tragedy have been avoided?

If you could turn back time

Ethan and Tina are planning to get married in less than a year. Tina is recommending they speak to a counselor about some of their issues.

Ethan: I am so excited we are getting married in 8 months. Things are working out just as I planned.

Tina: Ethan, seriously we need to talk. I spoke to my spiritual advisor and we need to speak to someone about our issues.

Ethan: What issues? We don't have any issues. So I grabbed your arm a little hard, I said I was sorry.

Tina: What does God say about how you should honor me? What does the Word say about you covering me as a wife?

Ethan: Don't throw scripture at me. I know the Bible like the back of my hand. You are to submit and I am to be the head of the house. Period!

Tina: If that is how you see a Godly marriage, we

really need help. God will not honor disobedience and I am not marrying you without counseling. Do you realize there is something wrong with this relationship?

Ethan: I don't have a problem. I don't think.

Ethan hesitates as he glares into Tina's eyes and realizes that she was not moving from her position. Ethan truly loves Tina. Over a course of 6 months Ethan enters an anger management program. The wedding was postponed for a year. We are proud to say, the couple is married to this day and a strong testimony to other couples of how you can recover in a storm.

Physical and verbal abuses are signals of low self esteem and suppressed anger. Abusive folks will migrate to peaceful and meek spirited individuals who show love and concern for everyone regardless of how they behave. The challenge for the meek spirited spouse is to hold his or her spouse accountable for their actions. This can be hard, but it needs to be done. Move away from a spirit of enablement, which encourages him or her to continue abusive behavior patterns. Transform your mind with the word of God and hold each other accountable as heirs of God's kingdom. Part of accountability is having honest and open conversations with each other.

Do not lose your "voice."

Not losing your voice means, you love your spouse enough to tell him or her truth. Calling on Jesus who understands your concerns and giving you the now time word to say in order for your spouse to be receptive. Additionally, seek out other strong Christian men and women who can reach your spouse. Release your pride and embrace those who can meet some of the areas that you cannot fulfill in your spouse.

Once you have voiced your concerns, you want to release your spouse to God and allow Him to work out the situation in them. The goal is not to throw up on your spouse but to speak truth and life into the situation. The reality is that you cannot be everything for your spouse. Only God can be everything all the time and in every situation.

From a Trifling Act to a Treasured Response: 2 Corinthians 1:4

God comforts us in all our troubles, so that we can comfort those in any trouble with the comfort we ourselves have received from God! When I have been under pressure, God is right there to give me assurance and encouragement. When you need confidence that He is working things out for your good and His glory, know that His Word will never fail. Having that confidence will help you move from faith to faith. You will move from a place of brokenness to a position of healing. Don't be like the man who sat by the pool for years, waiting for someone else to do something for him. The man sat waiting for the Angel to stir the water, waiting for someone to put him in the pool, waiting for a divine miracle on his behalf. (*John 5:6*) God is asking you to get up from your bed of issues and be free.

Ask yourself:
1. Do you want to be made whole?
2. Do you want your marriage to change for the better?
3. Do you want to live in the peace that only God can give you? God is waiting on you to do your part. God gives you the option of life or death. Choose life!

Trifling Act Scene 14:
Why are you so hateful?

Ever have one of those days, months, even years, where everything was a struggle? Struggling with a sick child; finally graduating from school, or drafting papers on a new home are all challenging events. You have thoughts of kicking the cat, biting the dog, or running butt naked in the street. In the same breath you half heartedly thank God that you survived the temptation to lose your mind. Instead of feeling relieved and truly thankful that the Lord brought you through, you are just as bitter and disappointed, allowing past pains to replay over and over in your mind. You are still up-tight and sensitive to old baggage from the past that you should have forgotten or lost by now. It is time to detoxify or rid yourself of the emotional baggage attached to problems you have already lived through. Your negative experiences are hindering your ability to enjoy the blessing God has for you.

Here is a suggestion, after you have prayed to the only one who can give you peace, which is God alone, try this little detoxification tip. Pamper yourself as a symbol of washing away the pain, frustration and aggravation. Get a pedicure, manicure, body massage, go golfing, or bowling, or all of the above. After the symbolic cleansing act, open your heart and respond to the Lord's voice. The Lord will open your mind to understand through His word. (*Luke 24:45*) Once you have cleaned out the negative- replace those negative thoughts with the affirming promises of hope and love. The devil attempts to replace your cleaned out spirit with seven demons greater than the original issue God delivered you from.

Concentrating on the negative will only assist you in the bitter adventure of staying that way. Functioning in the negative will keep you hateful. A hateful attitude can be associated with disappointments that were never resolved. When a man fails to honor and respect you, the betrayal can cripple your flesh and weaken your spirit. The reality is man will fail you each and every day in some way.

Placing the burden of perfection on your spouse will subject him/her to failure; and when he/she fails, you somehow feel justified in your disappointment and anger. Stop setting your spouse up to fail. The reality is that perfection does not exist in man but in Jesus Christ. When you let disappointment gain a solid foothold in your life you will disappoint yourself on occasion.

For example, you promised to leave work on time starting Monday, to spend time with your spouse who has asked and even begged for time with you. It is now Wednesday at 6:30 pm and you are at work. You arrive home to an icy reception from your spouse. You are surprised that he/she is not waiting for you with baited breath; so he/she failed you? You do not honor your own words with the ones you love. Admit it you have emotional baggage to unload, and quit holding on to problems out of your control! Reach out to God for the strength to ask for a healing in your heart and soul which will allow you to love in spite of the hurt you feel.

Anger is disappointment outwardly expressed. Satan's trick is to convince you that in order to vindicate yourself, you need to show your disappointment and distress. Just hateful! You are looking for an apology that may never come. If the apology never comes, what are you going to do? Living in the broken places of a relationship is nonproductive and destructive. If indeed the apology never occurs and forgiveness is never expressed know that God knows all things. Accept the fact that the very hurt you feel is what Jesus felt on the cross for your sake and mine. Bless God for the sacrifice of His son.

You become a witness of peace that emanates from a mind set on the Spirit of God. To be an effective witness requires expressing God's love to your un-loving spouse. When you cannot show love toward those that hurt you, your disobedience states you truly do not believe God represents you in all things and in all ways. The scripture says, *"What if some do not believe, does that make the faith of God without affect? God forbid. Let God be true and every man a liar"* (*Romans 3:3*). Just because you are travailing over the issues does not diminish God's capacity to deliver.

Isaiah 30:15 says that in quietness and confidence, God will be your strength. Living in confident assurance that God will deliver you from the very thing that hurts you, keeps you in perfect peace. Placing your heart and mind in a state of quiet reflection and meditation allows you to hear from God. The scripture says to lay aside every weight and the sin that so easily besets you (*Hebrews 12:1*). Just like an individual who lifts weights will test his or her muscles by taking on more weight, you take on more responsibilities by supporting your spouse and family.

A weight lifter will usually have a spotter or helper who will assist the lifter when he or she believes that they may be carrying something beyond their ability. The unique job of the spotter is to determine at what point to help the lifter with the weight. This means the spotter has to pay attention to when the lifter needs help!

The Holy Spirit is your spiritual spotter; he can help you with the weight, giving support to help you finish what you started. He also makes sure that you are not crushed by the heavy load. Your husband or wife can be your physical spotter, but they cannot help you if they cannot figure out what weight you need help with and what sin you should have dropped a long time ago.

Deliver me

Shauna has an issue with security. She marries Tyron. They have been married for 10 years. Shauna knew Tyron's medical practice was his passion. One of the things that impressed her most about Tyron was the compassion he demonstrated toward his patients. Prior to marrying Shauna, Tyron would schedule a special dinner for the two of them, only to stand her up for hours at the restaurant because a patient required assistance. Tyron did not have other doctors in his practice to give support and balance the patient schedule.

Today, Tyron has two other doctors to balance the work load in his practice. Financially, they are successful and prospering. After waiting 10 years to have some personal, intimate time with Tyron, Shauna is tired of spending her evenings alone while Tyron is off running around who knows where doing who knows what. Tyron has felt the tension in the home and instead of addressing it, he does not tell Shauna when he is invited to events and goes without her.

Tyron: My work is very important. You know that.

Shauna: So, I guess I am not important?

Tyron: That is not what I mean. You are twisting my words again and over reacting.

Shauna: I am not twisting your words. I want you to hear how your words sound to me- like an excuse.

Tyron: This is why I can't talk to you. This is why I can't take you anywhere. Everything is always a major issue and I don't want the hassle.

Shauna: So now I am a hassle. You didn't think I was a hassle last night in bed. Are you married to your practice or to me? I want to see you sleep with your desk!

Tyron: Of course I am married to you. But we need to eat which is why I need to work.

Shauna: Oh please, you have plenty of people to help you in the practice. You don't want to be home. I feel like a single parent raising our children.

The trifling conversation continues, which includes passing blame, defending a useless position and holding on to attitudes that are not productive. Both individuals are resentful and frustrated with the current condition of their marriage. Shauna considered the potential economic freedom that Tyron could afford.

But she did not count the cost of the freedom she was walking into. It is a known fact that living together before you get married distorts your ability to see your spouse completely. This is why it is important to look for spiritual characteristics over physical characteristics.

Shauna and Tyron lived together before they got married. When Shauna became pregnant Tyron married her in her fourth month of pregnancy. Why not marry her? He really did love Shauna. This couple is an excellent example of why cohabitation does not equate to a successful long lasting marriage. Playing house is just that "playing". It is not real; so the same issues you had while you were playing house just magnify when you get married.

Tyron thought Shauna understood his position. Tyron thought being married consisted of adding a ring to a lady's finger and continuing with his same lifestyle and attitude. Wrong, and wrong again! When a man does not show and behave in a manner that says, "Next to God, my wife is the most important person in my life", then the wife will continue to challenge her husband to validate where his priorities are.

From a Trifling Act to a Treasured Response: Romans 13:12

Replacing the hateful you with the glorified you will require discarding the dark side of your behavior. Set aside the deeds of darkness. Think for a moment about some of the unattractive actions you have performed in your marriage. How about when you left his golf shoes out in the rain? Remember the $150 Homeowner Association fine you paid last month, because you did not remove the trash can from the curb? Declare war on a sour attitude. Jesus defeated the dark side of your personality when He died on the cross. The situation you are in is only for a season. Do not make a permanent decision when you are in a temporary condition. Tomorrow will come and the sun will rise.

Identify what triggers your defensive attitude. Ask God to heal you from whatever gets in your way of demonstrating peace to your spouse. If that means you need to speak up earlier before an issue becomes explosive, do that!

Trifling Act Scene 15:
What's love got to do with it?

A few years ago Tina Turner asked us all, this question. Here is an excerpt from my letter in response to her question:

> Dear Miss Turner:
> Love has everything to do with it!
> Sincerely,
>   Shirley Lytle

Seriously though, love has everything to do with you, your marriage, and having the right fellowship with God. It has everything to do with the promise of peace that goes beyond your understanding. Love has everything to do with connecting with your wife.

However, before discussing how to improve your love communication, it is necessary to determine if you believe in love. But what is love? Love is more than words. It is a manifestation of God through you. We all have various interpretations of love. Let's review how God describes love.

Love is patient, love is kind. It does not envy, it does not boast, it is not proud. It always protects, always trusts, always hopes, and always perseveres. 1 Corinthians 13:4, 7.

Those of you who have been told by abusive spouses, parents, etc. that they abuse you because they love you; they are telling you a lie and the truth is not in them. Love, according to the world is attached to feeling good and having your way. Love is not hateful or harmful or degrading or anything less than God's exhibit of patience and kindness. If you don't feel protected then it is not love. If you can't trust the fact that God has placed this person in your life then it is not love. If you can't demonstrate long suffering for one another then it is not love. God so loved the world that he GAVE his only Son, Jesus, just for you. If you are one of God's children, you must love.

Now that you have a definition of real love, do you believe it?

Surprisingly, many men and women don't believe in this perfect expression of love. You know why? The devil has managed to turn love into a physical act instead of an act of service. Though the devil does not have dominion over the Children of God, Satan still has power on the earth. The enemy reaches you in your physical beings and manipulates the truth. He uses your trifling nature.....pure and simple.

The saved and sanctified men and women of God have relinquished their power to the devil. You have a casual or trifling attitude toward the power that love holds in your life. You have taken a trifling approach to the grace God has given you through the power of LOVE to heal and move in your purpose. You do not feel loved. However, there is nothing in the scripture that says that love is a feeling. Love believes in the Word of God. *Luke 10:19* talks about how Jesus has given us authority to trample on snakes and scorpions and to overcome all the power of the enemy. Nothing

90

and I mean nothing will harm you when you gird your mind and spirit in the love of the Lord.

Show me a husband or wife who truly believes in the Word of God and I will show you a spouse who knows how to love. If you do not believe you deserve to be loved, you cannot give true love. It will be conditional and physical in nature. Believe today that you deserve to be loved. Drop that trifling spirit that the power of love is not effective. You cannot give what you do not have. The power of love fueled by God, sacrificed Jesus on the cross and then raised Him from the dead. Loving and being loved as God intended shows commitment and dedication to others, especially your spouse.

The Decision to love

When Elena first met her husband, she made a point to find out what he liked, did not like and what made his "bell" ring! Paying close attention to his personal preferences in food, clothing and church music was paramount to successfully finding favor in the eyes of Chris. After the wedding, Elena's focus transitioned from Chris to making a house, a living, a family and a career. Over the past 2 years, Elena feels disconnected from Chris. They rarely have any personal time with each other. Elena attends the women's Bible study at church. The teacher introduced a book called "Five Love Languages" by Gary Chapman. Elena brings the book home and a family discussion ensues.

Can you speak my language?

91

Elena: Do you know what I need the most?
Between reading his newspaper and watching the news, Chris murmurs, "what?"

Elena: This book says that what I ask of you the most is what motivates me.

Chris: What book, and what are you talking about?

Elena: Quality Time, Words of Affirmation, Receiving Gifts, Acts of Service and Physical Touch. I think my love language is Words of Affirmation.

Chris: No, your love language is receiving gifts!

Elena: Just how would you know what I like? You just give me the credit card and say have fun!

Chris: Isn't that what every woman wants, an unlimited credit card option?

A painful pregnant pause is felt and Chris realizes his wife is really trying to find a way to connect with him. The couple spends a month reading the book and determining what each other's love language really is. The only rule relative to demonstrating each other's love language is that they could not spend more than $50 a month. Additionally, if either of them tried a language that did not meet the other's need, it was important to ask the following questions:

- What do you need the most?
- What makes you feel the most loved?
- What hurts you deeply?
- What do you desire most of all?

Learning each other's love language has improved their ability to speak in a way that the other can respond to in a positive manner. Elena's primary love language is "Words of Affirmation and her secondary love language is "Receiving Gifts". Chris's primary love language is "Acts of Service" and his secondary love language is "Physical Touch". The couple moved from a stagnant position in their relationship to a place of focusing on each other's need and the intrigue of continually finding new ways to express their love for each other in the language each wanted and needed.

Love has everything to do with how your spouse feels loved, respected and honored in the relationship. In order to really love someone you need to give of yourself. Consider the selfless act of Jesus. Jesus suffered when He was tempted, yet he was able to help those who were being tempted. Love is a choice. Love makes a difference. Love must be sincere. Hate what is evil and cling to what is good. Choosing to love in the language of your spouse has many benefits. It will help heal past wounds and provide a sense of security, selfworth and significance in your marriage.

There is a difference between merely falling in love with the idea of love and making the choice to love for life. *"God has not given us a spirit of fear, but of love, power and a sound mind"* (2 *Timothy 1:7*). A sound mind is a disciplined mind. Develop a strategy that will show your spouse that your mind, body and spirit are disciplined to the point that nothing will shake your commitment to each other.

From a Trifling Act to a Treasured Response: 1 John 4:8- 12

If you love Jesus, prove it- love back. The greatest opportunity to demonstrate the love of God manifested

93

on the earth is through your acts of kindness, peace, gentleness and longsuffering. God is love. You are His child, which means you have the ability to love just as strong. Sacrificial love says my spouse's needs are considered above my own. Unconditional love means you accept your spouse the way he or she is as God works on their transformation. Agape love is an act of will. We are not capable of being God. However, you are the product of an all mighty God created in Christ Jesus. God gave us Jesus as an example of true love.

1. What will you do today to show your spouse you truly love him or her?
2. How have you demonstrated longsuffering in your relationship?
3. Where is God leading you to release an arrogant and prideful spirit?
4. Have you released the desire to keep record of all the hurt and shame in your marriage?

Trifling Act Scene 16:
The Good, the Bad and the Ugly

Here's the deal. Bad things happen to good people; good things happen to bad people and bad things happen to bad people. The ugly truth is that the rain falls on the just and the unjust. The question posed to the child of God is, "Do you believe God has predestined your steps for greatness?"(*Ephesians 1:11*) Believing that God set you apart for a specific destiny will give you strength to continue to persevere in times of trouble.

Those bad things may happen in your own church family. Many couples in the church struggle to reach out for help within the church because their business gets out in the street......somehow. They are shocked and dismayed that their situation is preached during the 11 o'clock service or discussed during Wednesday night Bible study. Believe this if you will, but church folk are not always walking in the light of the Lord.

Everyone is a work in process and we pray that they progress into what God would have them to be. There are "information seekers" who do not realize the immaturity they exhibit when they become a distributor of gossip, instead of praying for hurting Christians.

Yes, it is unfortunate that everyone that goes to church is not looking for Jesus. Without going into detail, individuals who crowd a church have a multitude of reasons for their attendance. The church was never meant to be a dating service or a social club, but a place to find refuge in Jesus.

Many churchgoers are too busy putting on their make up or text messaging their next conquest in the pews before the benediction is pronounced. There are men who come to church looking for a "holy hug" from a woman: which is a hug where the bodies meet from the knees to the neck and there is not enough room to slide a piece of paper between the two and the embrace is 'just a little longer' than is comfortable.

Discernment is important when working inside and outside of the church. God gives us a spirit of discernment in order to separate those spirits that come to us. Don't get it twisted! Know there is an enemy out there with a primary goal to kill, steal and destroy one's connection and communion with God. Understand that the devil is actively seeking ways to tear down marriages. Yet with all the rumblings going on in the church today, couples continue to get married believing that "the power of love" will see them through.

Love is a choice. Love is a sign of obedience to God. Loving this way takes strength outside of who you are. Love requires taking God at His Word at all times. When you take someone at his or her word, you may struggle with releasing authority over the issue. You trust God, but you do not trust yourself to wait on God to work the situation out!

If you cannot trust yourself, how can you trust anyone else? *Matthew:12* proposes that the good in you will produce good and the evil within you will produce evil. Understanding the good, the bad and the ugly that reside in you will resurrect those things that require healing, discarding and/or building up.

There is a freedom that resonates from a man or woman of God who knows where he or she is going, even if that destination is a trip one day at a time. It is paramount to learn from the spiritual trip God walks you through and return with a positive witness. When your marriage is in a crisis, it is really good to pray. However, the Word states you must pray and do something about your situation. Faith without works is dead. If your husband needs to see a doctor, prayer works as well as getting him to a hospital. Act on what will edify God. Move in the direction of change for the better not the worse.

Losing sleep concentrating on the negative situations in your life will only result in circles under your eyes. Rise up from your oppression and put God's Word on the problem. Why not meditate on what is good, what is pleasant and what is of good report? You will not gain even a moment in time concentrating on what could go wrong. Take dominion over your life and your marriage. Declare that the devil will not take your husband, your wife, or a family member.

Over time you have given the devil more power than the Lord ever expected. It is time to take back what the devil has stolen. You do not have time to list the ways your spouse is not meeting your needs and expectations. Meditate on what God has charged you to accomplish and correct. Consider how the children of Israel felt when they finally arrived to the land of promise. They were persuaded in their own minds that they could not overtake the city. Why? Because they concentrated on the negative, and the giant sized enemy. They could not conceive possessing their promise.However, if the enemy was so great, how in the world did they get into the city and bring back evidence of the fruit within the land? There are times when all you need is the tenacity and a window of opportunity to take what God has already promised to you.

Do you feel me?

Melissa and David are ready to have a baby. Yet, the conception piece is not working fast enough for Melissa.

After three years of marriage and one full year of trying, Melissa knew it was her turn to get pregnant and have a baby. The doctor said there was nothing wrong with her or her husband David. The doctor stated that if she was not pregnant in a year that other options could be identified to help their progression. After six months, David's enthusiasm is weaning. He is beginning to doubt if indeed they would ever have a baby. Yet Melissa's faith was unwavering. The desire to have a baby was taking a toll on their relationship. David wanted to give up trying so hard and Melissa was getting her second wind to endure to the end. The couple met with Darryl and me to receive encouragement and sound counsel regarding their situation. The following is the dialogue that ensued.

David: I just don't think we need to eat, sleep and think 24/7 about having a baby. I am beginning to believe all she sees me as is a baby machine.

Melissa: That is not true. I just want God to know that I took Him at His Word and we are going to have a baby. Not to mention the fact, everyone seems to be getting pregnant but us.

David: We rarely go out to fellowship with other people anymore. It is as if everything has stopped until we have a baby. I am not having it. She gets depressed every time we walk by someone who has a child.

Melissa sits silently as David continues to describe a pattern of obsession with getting pregnant. She begins to cry and David now feels he has gone too far with his observations. This scene is common with couples who desire to have a baby and the time does not come fast enough or may never come. Waiting on your promise land to arrive can be a painful experience. Melissa has made the event of getting pregnant a chore instead of connecting emotionally and physically with David. The Word says that God will give you rest. When Melissa stated she believed God for a baby, she needs to rest in the belief that regardless of what occurs or does not occur each month God is working it out for her good and His glory. The Word places you in a position of rest.

Believing for your blessing and running to make it happen on your own will make you tired and frustrated. Lack of rest will result in exposing vulnerable places within you. Fatigue and restlessness in a person will lead to irritation and frustration.

Let's take a look at some other examples that cause stress and strain on a relationship:

- Supporting your adult children who are not doing anything for themselves.
- Living off a budget that is so tight that you have to ask for permission to purchase toilet paper.

- Working three jobs for a year to make ends meet without a word of support from your spouse.

All of the above can cause unrest physically, which will then leave you exposed for a spiritual attack. These are examples of how you have tried to fix a problem with your own will and in your own timeline. Resting in the promises of God alters the atmosphere by providing balance that will calm your spirit and keep you physically in a place of rest. Know that He who has begun a good work in you will complete it (*Philippians 1:6*). Rushing God will cause you unrest. When you do not believe that your spouse is not making changes fast enough or your finances are not clearing up quick enough, know God is not a God of confusion. That is the devil's job to cause confusion.

Rest in knowing God is true to His Word. Heaven and earth will pass away before God's word could ever fail. When you pray, God will answer. Walk in faith until your answer manifests itself in the natural.

From a *Trifling* Act to a Treasured Response: Romans 8:28

Regardless of the environment you are living in, decide to enjoy the journey. Over the past 45 years of my life, I have learned to enjoy the journey. I have spent too many sleepless nights trying to get my situation to change. I have lost joy. I have lost peace. God never meant for you to live defeated. All things do work together for good, even if it does not appear that the result is good. God's timing is not my timing, yet His will is what I live to understand. When you know that you know that all things work together for good, you will enjoy the journey.

1. How do you release the stress in your life? (Other than throwing your family out of the house.)

2. Being married does not mean losing who you are. What steps are you taking to remain your unique self and support your family?

Trifling Act Scene 17:
And the wheels on the bus go round and round

How many times are you and your spouse going to go round and round an issue before there is resolution? Darryl and I are firm believers in having a strong argument about an issue. The real problem we have with arguing is when it does not produce a positive solution, or people don't resolve the issue. You spend so much energy and effort trying to prove your spouse wrong in an area, that you miss the opportunity to be understood.

How many times does the Lord have to bring you to your knees about a situation? How often must God allow a situation to recur in your life before you say "Enough Lord!" Determine to stop running from what the Lord is trying to teach you and move on to the greater things God has for your marriage.

Help, I need somebody

Help me understand how you can say you love God, but can't stand to be around your spouse. Help me understand how you can help your neighbor, but allow your spouse to handle all the calls from the collectors. Help me understand why you attend every church event, but cannot spend time with your spouse. Help me understand why Jesus who set you free when He died on the cross, cannot loose the bonds strangling your marriage. Help me understand!

Couples experience paralysis believing God is part of their marriage. They do not see God working in their husband or wife fast enough for them. You go to church, you hear the messages of love, peace and faith, and you go home. Converting the message heard during the service becomes a battle of validation with your spouse. The battle field consists of the couple, God and the Devil. Stop treating your spouse as the enemy; accept him or her as a part of your defense. You bring into marriage an anointing which allows you to defend what God has given you authority to protect. You change physically and spiritually because of the anointing God placed on the inside of you. What you do with the gift inside of you must be motivated by a passion to please God not man. It takes God's power to do God's work in a marriage. Like the dating game mentioned previously, you marry someone, and then you attempt to change the nature of the person. God actually placed you with that person to allow you're anointing to grow, not to point out what is wrong with your spouse.

Lesson learned

My ability to speak into the life of other couples did not truly begin to develop until God began to speak to me about my own marriage. The gift placed within was in a seed form early in my marriage. Christ stands for "the Anointed One". Jesus was described as the Christ because he was the anointed one sent from God! God sent you to be an anointed gift to your spouse. God revealed to me how being "right" was not always

104

"alright". The scripture says that a wife should have such a reverence for her husband that she is in awe of him. I asked God if He was making jokes because of that issue in the garden. Be in awe of a man? Yet, if you live long the Lord will bless you to live through the great and the small issues of life in order to see your own evolution.

I experienced God transforming me and not my husband. My transformation allowed me to see Darryl de-robed before my eyes as the magnificent man of God I honor today. There is a powerful victory to celebrate when you have a break through from an issue God has delivered you from.

There comes a time in your relationship where you decide that one day the very grace you are withholding from your spouse will one day be the grace you will demand from your spouse.

It would be easy to find a few friends that would agree with your current view point of 'you are so right and they are so wrong or how can you put up with such mess?' However, you are not married to them. You need to work **your** issues out with **your** spouse. Seek out Christians who will challenge how you process your thoughts about the situation. You need an accountable prayer partner who will bring correction; charge you to repent, and turn from the easy appearance of evil, and look to God for the *Right* answers!

I no longer desire to be right, I want to be free. I need the sustaining power of God in my life. "Being Free" means to posses a desire to line up with God's Word and His will over and beyond my own desire. Being free outweighs your desire to be right in your own mind; in discord with your husband and out of order with God. Lining up with God's agenda requires obedience. Obedience is better than sacrifice, obey God. Decide to become tired of dealing with the same issues over and over again. I had plenty of problems that I continued to circle around and around.

An example of my disobedience centers on my mouth. In moments of frustration with Darryl during our early years of marriage, I would use foul language to get my point across. I thank God for delivering me from the cursing spirit that consumed my mouth in my younger years. I would find reasons to use this cursing spirit to justify why I had to resort to such vulgar communication to get my point across. It was God's sustaining power that helped me see the error of my ways, but not without 'Pimp' Satan trying to condemn my efforts. The devil would attempt to play with my head regarding God and my husband being able to forgive me, by planting seeds of deception.

When you want to be free, more than you want to be right, you will open your mouth and shout loudly for the grace of God to cover all sin through Jesus, the intercessor, which sits next to God himself. Transition and change are what God does best in your life. At some point, you must be willing to stop the insanity. Insanity is doing the same thing over and over again and expecting a different result. Transition may be painful; however it does get you out of the rut you are currently living in.

Running round and round like a hamster going nowhere even frustrates the animal in the cage. Decide to get off the circular treadmill and do a new thing in your marriage. Pimp Satan wants to trick you into believing that through your own strength you can make

106

an impact. Your approach and methods will require change in order to meet the emotional and physical needs of your spouse. As I mentioned earlier having a strong disagreement or argument concerning the life of your marriage is healthy. It says you are passionate enough about your marriage that you are willing to have an altercation to move into a clarifying moment. The non-productive activity is when you do not change your method or approach and your communication is not effective.

From a *Trifling* Act to a Treasured Response: Hebrews 10:24-25

In order to determine how to stir one another up, you will need to spend time taking inventory on your spouse. You have the ability to draw out the good works hidden in your spouse. Plan a weekly date night. Neglecting your spouse on a regular basis will result in losing touch with his or her uniqueness. Problems cannot be resolved without communication that leads to a greater understanding of each other. Make a concerted effort to be the resident expert on your spouse. The same amount of time and energy that you exert playing basketball or researching a new hairstyle, place on learning something new about your spouse.

Trifling Act Scene 18:
He made me do it!

No one can make you do anything. Let me repeat. No one makes you raise your voice, hold a grudge or lift a finger unless you allow it. Your friends did not force you to pierce your ear lobe or go to a strip club. You decided to go and put the money in some stripper's foreign piece of underwear. Now that's real. No one makes you beat your spouse. This act of insecurity is from the pit of hell and needs to be rebuked and eradicated from the body of Christ.

The whole excuse game was first played out in the Garden of Eden. "The woman you gave me caused me to eat." Try another line Adam, it didn't work back then and it is not working now. The promise or covenant was spoken directly to Adam (not Eve) and he was accountable to it.. Every choice you have made and every step you have taken has your name on it. You own it and the consequences attached to the actions you've taken. You live in a society that says everything that goes wrong with you is someone else's fault. It is not longer your responsibility. The trouble with this concept is that unless you take responsibility for your actions, there can be no real healing of the mind and spirit. When a marriage comes to an end, it is important for each party to identify where he or she went wrong in the relationship.

Did I learn a lesson?

Marsha and Craig were married for 25 years. They have two children that are now on their own and making a good living. Six months ago the marriage was officially terminated by divorce. The decision to divorce came as a shock to the church congregation. The couple appeared to be just fine. Looks can be deceiving! Six months after the divorce, Craig is now seeking premarital counseling. He is marrying the woman he committed adultery with. As they sat in our family room the hundred dollar question came up.

Darryl: What part did you play in the failing of your last marriage?

Craig: I do not see what that has to do with my marriage to Tina.

Tina: I think he was never in love with his ex-wife and I gave him what he needed.

The problem with Craig's rationale is that he will repeat the same poor behavior if he does not understand his contribution to the failure of his previous marriage. Tina could be the next recipient of an unfaithful event.

Craig: My ex-wife was never home. She was too busy with the children and I never had access to a healthy sex life.

Again the question was restated: What did you do to save your marriage?

Craig: There was no reason to save the marriage. She was never going to change.

We directed the next question to Tina.

110

Darryl: What would you do if Craig has an affair with someone? Are you willing to be faithful in the marriage?

Tina: Craig would not do that to me. He loves me. (With a nervous undertone)

Craig: Tina is a different woman than my ex-wife.

Darryl: Are you willing to take accountability for your part in Craig's divorce?

Tina: Craig approached me. I did not approach him. I did not know until much later that Craig was married with children. I admire him because he waited until all his children were grown before he divorced his wife.

There were red flags waving all over the place. Craig did not take accountability for any part of the failed marriage. He did not want to accept the fact that he took no active role in raising their children. As a matter of fact, Craig's oldest son has known for about four years that his father was unfaithful to his mother. Yet that did not cause any conviction on Craig's part to confess and seek marriage counseling for their failed relationship. I know we are focusing on Craig right now, but Marsha would be challenged the same way to identify where she failed in the marriage. Likewise Tina is in a fantasy land regarding her contribution and Craig's dedication to upholding the marriage bed.

When a marriage does not succeed, there are two people in the equation- 50% of the responsibility is his and 50% of the responsibility is hers. Additionally, much like the Garden of Eden, there will always be a snake in the equation as well. Even in times where there is abuse either verbally or physically, each individual plays a part in the failure of the relationship. You may say how is that? In the case of physical abuse, when the first hand was lifted against you, that should have been your wake-up call that this person is not for you. You saw the signs before you were married that he was overly aggressive and possessive, yet you married him.

In the case of abuse, the snake resembles denial and embarrassment which hinders your ability to seek out help. God loves you so much that He speaks to your heart to let you know the road ahead is going to be rough. Yet, the Lord will not overrule your own will. Your spouse should love and appreciate you for the jewel you are in Christ. Not for what you look like in a Speedo.

Your flesh nature has too many flaws to be trusted with the will of God. People cannot appreciate who you are because they are still struggling to move beyond who they are. Let me clarify, Craig grew up with a domineering mother, who orchestrated his every move. In his first marriage, Craig swore that he would wear the pants in the house. His ex-wife was a caring individual, until she woke up one morning feeling overwhelmed and unappreciated by her husband. Craig incorporated his fears into his marriage. Suppressed anger and frustration deposited into a marriage strains your ability to articulate in a loving and caring way. Every individual walks into a relationship with issues. The question is do you know the issues you bring to the table and are you willing to work them out? If you do fall down, get up and learn from the experience. Learn to say "I'm sorry" and really mean it.

From a *Trifling* Act to a Treasured Response: Proverbs 3:13

Happy is a man who finds wisdom and who acquires understanding. What is wisdom? "It's so simple to be wise. Just think of something stupid to say and say the opposite."- Sam Levinson

A happy person is one who searches for wisdom in his or her life. A happy marriage is built on continually finding a new awareness of your spouse. Whether you have been married for one week or 30 years, a lesson can be learned each day. What have you learned new about your spouse over the past week, month, year? God's mercies are renewed daily, so should your view on how to love and support one another, be renewed daily. Life is more than being married, it is about living married. Learning from previous mistakes and adjusting your approach accordingly can help you move forward instead of backward in your marriage.

Trifling Act Scene 19: Respect this!

D o you recall where you lost it? Respect for your spouse, do you remember? You loved him or her enough to marry them, but now you do not value him or her enough to show respect. As a matter of fact, you show more respect to the mail man when he delivers the mail each day. More words are spoken to a stranger than to your spouse. Why, because she or he was working your nerves last night. This respect thing is significant in a household. When we take advantage of one another, eventually, a breakdown occurs in the relationship. Respect is an intricate part of a man's self esteem. Articulating your appreciation for your wife's contributions encourages more cooperation.

More than what you see

About two years ago, Joel and Annette agreed for Annette to quit her job and spend more time pursuing her college degree. Annette was excited for this opportunity. Leaving her job and living on one income demonstrated their confidence in God taking care of their every need through Joel's job. The Lord was truly blessing this couple in all areas. The children are well and the new home was finally decorated. Yet, all is not well in paradise.

Over a period of one year, sickness began to afflict the family. Health issues can take more than money to mend. Annette had two surgeries, which were debilitating in nature. It was difficult to lift heavy objects and she easily became fatigued during the day. There were daily reminders that Annette was no longer herself. With and through the pain, Annette willed herself to function as she previously performed. She continued to go to school, take care of the household choirs and rip and run to every event the children were scheduled to attend. Joel was so busy with his work and making a living that he missed the "cues" that Annette gave off on a daily basis. She was tired or could not lift the laundry basket up the stairs anymore. Though the children were old enough to help and support her at home, Annette took on a martyr mentality instead of seeking the very support that was at her disposal.

Joel could sense the changing attitude of his wife but, figured if he ignored it, the problem would go away. Annette was drowning in the sea of "I want, I need and I got to have"!

Annette: I want a separation.

Joel: What! Where did this come from? What is this all about?

Annette: This family does not respect me and you do not help the situation. I am sick and tired of being sick and tired.

Joel: What do you mean we do not respect you? I come home everyday. I bring my paycheck home. You don't have to work. You have a brand new house and you can buy what you want.

Annette: Thank you for describing me like a prostitute that is being paid by the week for her services! I am more than what I do for this family. You need a maid not a wife.

Joel is stunned by the graphic description Annette provided regarding what she believes she represents in their relationship.

Joel: Do you need to go to the doctor? Maybe they had you under anesthesia too long and the medicine affected your thinking.

Annette: Let's see how many jokes you make when you are paying child support on a monthly basis. I hurt every day and no one cares. I run your dang errands and attend the children events to the point that by the end of the day I have been in and out of the car so much that I can't even sit when I get home.

Joel realizes that he has missed the mark and Annette realizes that this is the first time she has had a real honest conversation about her issues to Joel. Men do not read minds or tea leaves! Annette has some valid concerns. Every person requires and should expect a little "me" time. It allows for rejuvenation and recovery. Even if that "me" time is an hour or two each day. Find it or someone will find a purpose for your "me" time without you.

Is it possible that because Annette continued to press beyond her pain and continues to function as if nothing was wrong that Joel ignored the obvious signs that Annette was suffering? Is it possible that Joel is taking Annette's contributions for granted because she is a stay-at -home mom? Is it obvious that these two have lost touch of why God placed them in each other's lives? And let the church say AMEN!

Respect, respect, respect! It is a small word that holds great significance in a relationship, but is overlooked on a regular basis. We may remember Jacob's wives thought so little of him that Rebecca and Leah negotiated a night's sleep over a mandrake plant. **Trifling!** Let's apply this concept to Annette. She has lost her purpose in life now that she is no longer attached to a job or an organization. The lesson here: You have to respect yourself, if you expect others to respect you. Women suffer with self esteem issues on a regular basis. When you fail to know your purpose in life, you will sabotage your future and may not know why.

1Chronicles 29:11-12 states that everything in Heaven and Earth belongs to the Lord. I shall adore Him for being in control of everything.

Repeat after me:

Who am I?	God's Baby!
Where do I belong?	God's Kingdom!
Who has control?	God has control over everything!

What God has for me is for me. He has control over it all. The Lord told Jeremiah that He knew him before Jeremiah was born. God knew me before I messed up. Circumstances will hit you that make you wonder if you are even fit to represent God. Having a baby out of wedlock; a spiteful spirit; a carnal Christian. The Lord said He has a destiny for you. So He knows your issues, pains and victories. He knows some of the crazy things you have done and will do! In spite of that He still chose you. Put the Word of God that cannot fail to work on your situation. Keep reading your Bible about your entitlement as a child of God until you believe it.

You were born with an assignment just like Moses was called with an assignment on his life to free the Israelites. Even when the Devil tries to kill your first dream, don't worry, God has your back. The Lord is all knowing. He even planned for weaknesses in your flesh. Just because there are times your actions are in the flesh does not negate your obligation to what God has called you to do.

Growing into your anointing is just that- a growth process. You can grow up big and strong because you had your Cheerios, read the Word, and then apply the Word. Or you can grow up feeble because you have never stepped out on your anointing. The devil wants us to be bound, broke and defeated by the many fleshly actions we have taken. We feel unworthy to do God's will. God has placed gifts in you that you need to open your blinded eyes to. Believe your God is a God that can not fail. You need to show up with two things to grow into your anointing. Show up with faith and obedience. God will take care of the rest. The Lord chose us before the creation of the world. He predestined us to be adopted as his sons and daughters through Jesus Christ. (*Ephesians 1:4, 5*). I know who I am. I know whose I am, do you?

You are more than what others see!

You are more than what other people see! That in itself is a word. I will use myself as an example. I am more than what you see. I stand before you as a child of God. I am the wife of Darryl Lytle. I am the mother of David Lytle. I am the daughter of Nathan and Elaine Smith. I support the efforts of couples to stay strong in their marriages. I am a co-minister for the Marriage Enrichment Ministry at Pilgrim Rest Baptist Church, and Marriage and Family Enrichment of the Full Gospel Baptist Church Fellowship for the State of Arizona. I am more than what you see. Last but not least, I am a "wanna-be" comedian.

Start believing that the God who formed you in your mother's womb has plans for you that are greater than what you can see!

If I let the world determine my destiny, I would not have the intestinal fortitude (that means guts), to write this book. Because some people like to categorize individuals and put them on a shelf as decoration instead of using what is inside of the individual! Just as important, I must grow into what God has for me.

Growing into your own anointing, not someone else's is a powerful evolution. In other words, I was not called to sing. Not that I can't sing; I come from a family of singers. I receive comfort from singing. However, my passion, my direction, my talent is talking; a lot! Your anointing has a copyright, a unique stamp for you alone. Now be careful, because as women, we can do several things extremely well at one time. Have you ever seen a mother or a businesswoman function? You can clean the baby's nose and cook the chicken and dress your husband at the same time. As a businesswoman, you can complete the forecast for the business, take a complaint call and encourage an employee at the same time. Yet, whether you are taking care of the children or facilitating a staff meeting, God has placed a special gift inside of you to fulfill. What is that in you? This gift may not be obvious to others out in the world and in some cases it may not even be obvious to you, but you have a gift and purpose given to you by God.

Once you begin to believe that God has placed something in your spirit to accomplish, get ready. Now it's on with the Devil, his goal is to kill, steal and destroy that dream, that gift or purpose. Do not let the world determine the depth and the length of your existence. Pimp Satan tries to get you busted and disgusted so that you give up. In *Genesis 1:26 "God said, Let us make man in our image, in our likeness. So God created man in His own image, in the image of God he created him, male and female he created them."* You were made in the image and likeness of God. Get out of thinking of yourself in one dimension. You live in a body. You possess a soul, but your true nature is a spirit. Thinking in the flesh dimension limits your ability to take hold of the power of God in your life.

Each time there was a hater trying to weigh me down, to keep me in the flesh dimension; God would send someone who loved the anointing placed on my life to continue to speak truth into my spirit. Praise God. Paul stated God's spirit was deposited in our hearts guaranteeing what is to come. God guarantees that the work that the Lord has begun in you will be completed in His time and in His order. Waiting on that time and order is our daily struggle. But I urge, challenge and pray that nothing will separate you from your predestined future in God.

From a *Trifling* Act to a Treasured Response: 2 Corinthians 1:21, 22

(NIV) *"Now it is God who makes both us and you stand firm in Christ. He **anointed us**, set his seal of **ownership** on us, and put His Spirit in **our hearts** to deposit, guaranteeing what is to come."* You have been anointed, sealed and filled with His Spirit, to do more for His Kingdom. You have all the markings of a child of God.

In the Bible, Peter thought he had his position with Jesus all sown up. Peter's stronghold was that he did not know himself. *Luke 22:31-33*. Peter said he would go to prison and
to death with Jesus. He would later have a reality check with himself.

1. How do you define who you are? Job status, money, affiliations, etc.
2. Which characteristics would define the real you?
   Take the time to define yourself without the use of your status, money or accomplishments.
3. How does your purpose line up with the image of Jesus? (*Romans 8:29*)

Trifling Act Scene 20: Is your flesh ruling your actions?

When your flesh is dictating your every move and it feels good to be in a place of emotional destruction, you have officially "fleshed out!" Fleshed out means your behavior is well beyond the realm of Godly. Like a tea kettle ready to whistle, you are ready to give your spouse a piece of your mind that you can afford to lose. The children have run for cover, your husband has turned his hearing aid off and there you go. The words coming out of your mouth are not constructive or informational.

Once the words are released into the atmosphere, it is difficult to take them back and even more of a challenge to assist in the damage inflicted on the potential victim. I say potential victim because blame has the opportunity of being embraced by anyone in the line of fire. Moving from a flesh reaction to a spiritual response is a growing experience. God can see your motives and intentions as you prime your lips to speak words of direction and encouragement or words that will mutilate your mate.

Encountering growing pains

There is no getting around the pains associated with growing into the wife or husband God designed you to be. The process is what validates why God declares you as His child. The power of God commands your flesh to come under submission. God has empowered you with the Holy Spirit to combat your desire to manipulate your spouse. Your faith must move into the spirit realm in order to visualize your spouse as the divine woman or man of God. (*2 Corinthians 10:4*). If you continue to see your husband as the enemy, you can not unite with him to fight the original deceiver-Satan! The weapon of choice to use when shedding naughty habits in your life is GOD. Cut it out! Get a grip on yourself and your thoughts. Obey the Word as it relates to supporting your spouse. Remember obedience is better than sacrifice. The fact that you go to work everyday and bring back your paycheck is not a sacrifice. That is your reasonable service to supporting your family.

Moving from a fleshed out position to a selfless position in Christ will require reconciling with the enemy within you. The strongholds, the grips of disobedience allow you to revert to your "old nature". A stronghold is an area of resistance to the will of God. A stronghold is a place in the mind where you have allowed the devil to invade and occupy. When the devil has you by the mind he then has you by your dreams! Pimp Satan will use the habits you are struggling with against you. You cannot allow your flesh to dictate and impact your life. The flesh feeds off of fear.

Fear is a human weapon that the devil uses to bind your soul. Fear shows up in various forms within an individual. Second-guessing yourself, bitter feelings of inadequacies and throwing your own self under the little yellow short bus are elements of fear. Fear that is

124

not rebuked by the Word will develop into a stronghold. What you can't do, what you can't say and what you have never done does not matter to God. In the Bible, Sarah had a hollow womb, but God said that was not His stronghold. God can do all things. When Jeremiah told God he was a child, God said, I'll give you the words to speak! Both of these Biblical examples illustrate how thoughts regulate your forward mobility in Christ.

Ruled by the flesh

Donna is happily married to Calvin. They have two children and believe God has planted a great mission in their lives. Donna prides herself in taking good care of her children. After the last child, Donna battles with losing 30 pounds of "baby fat". Calvin does not care, because he loves her regardless of her size. Yet it is becoming a challenge for the couple to get beyond.

Donna: We should take the children to the park. It is a great day in the Lord to have lunch outside.

Calvin: That is a great idea. Let's get our swim suits on. I think there is a pool there as well.

Donna: I changed my mind. I don't feel like going out today.

Donna's demeanor changed quickly when she realized that she would be exposed in a bathing suit.

Calvin: Honey, what is the matter?
Donna: Nothing.

Calvin: Whenever you say nothing...it means some thing! What is wrong?

Donna: You know I can't wear a bathing suit. I am too fat!

Calvin: I love you just the way you are.

Donna: You have to say that. You have no other choice; you're bound to me for life.

Donna has a stronghold with her self-esteem. A cancer that plagues many men and women is their physical image. God designed you as a unique individual. Weight, height, and color hue does not dictate who you are inside. You have heard the joke about the individual who is described as having a great personality, but he or she must be ugly! The really ugly person is the individual who does not work on those personality traits that do not line up with exhibiting God's loving kindness.

If Peter really knew himself and knew that his faith was predicated on what he could see in the physical instead of the embodiment of who Jesus was he would not have denied Jesus. It is always good to know when Satan is attempting to sift you, to separate you from your true nature of God. You will make the mistake of thinking too highly of yourself! You will be like Peter and realize that you really don't know everything about the "You" in "YOU". When the attack comes your faith kicks in to deny the lie instead of your fears kicking in to believe Satan. Satan thinks so little of man that he thinks he can cut you down like wheat. But when you have Jesus as your mediator: your intercessor praying on your behalf, there's no way you can lose the fight against your flesh.

God will send people in your life that know your heart and see the anointing God has placed in your spirit. LISTEN TO THEM! This way when those who want to hold you back come along with their rhetoric, you will know whom to ignore! Know yourself in order to deal with the external opportunities. This will keep you from being overcome by the critics that the devil will bring your way. It will also help you realize when you have become a legend in your own MIND.

On with the story

Calvin loves his wife more than he loved being right. He knew there was nothing he could do, but encourage his wife. He also knew that this was something about how Donna saw herself, not just her weight. One year he purchased a fitness program for her, hoping that would motivate Donna to exercise. Oh it helped her exercise alright...her lungs. Donna screamed, hollered and then cried herself to sleep. Calvin realized quickly that the fitness membership was not the wisest birthday gift to present to his wife.

During this recent argument, Calvin saw the sheer desperation in his wife's face. He had to do something. Prayer is a powerful way to connect with your spouse. That evening, he asked Donna to pray with him.

Calvin: Lord, we thank you for all your many blessing. Most importantly, I thank you for the gift you have given me through Donna. Allow me to be a better husband and supporter of all she does. Amen

The next evening, Calvin was determined to reach Donna by any means necessary. After dinner, he loaded the children up in their favorite wagon and announced the family was taking a "family stroll". Every evening, regardless of how tired he was or Donna complained, the entire family took a walk. At first it was around the block, then down the street. After about four weeks, Donna actually could see change in her body. Calvin also encouraged her to take the children to daycare two days a week to give Donna some "me time".

Philippians 1:6 talks of how God will continue to develop and perfect you until you are completed in all areas. Press past the pain. Press past some of the ups and downs of growing out of your flesh and into your spirit man and woman of God. At this stage in your life, believe God has His hand on you.

From a *Trifling* Act to a Treasured Response: Proverbs 8:22

The Lord made you at the beginning of His creation, before His works of long ago. You were formed before the ancient times, from the beginning, before the earth began. This scripture is so powerful for the believer, for the redeemed of God. God sent His Son to die on a cross in order to redeem you from sin and shame. Do not allow the devil to use your flesh as a weapon of mass destruction. Refuse to allow the devil to deceive, distort and distract the original plans God has already established for your life. Identify areas that you are your worst enemy. Ask God to renew your mind. Turn your cares over to Him.

Trifling Act Scene 21:
Don't judge me by my strongholds

Have you ever heard the church described as a hospital? Yes, the church can be categorized as a hospital. In the same way a hospital has various levels of wounded or sick patients, a church welcomes various levels of wounded and healed Christians. There are emergency room doctors, specialized physicians, critically ill and volunteers. There are people dying and people recovering from surgery. The sanctuary has several types and conditions of individuals entering every Sunday. There are people with broken hearts, spousal abuse, lonely hearts and enthusiastic disciples. The first question you must ask yourself is what condition are you in when you enter the church house? The next question, do you have a specialist working on your case or is another sick person trying to help you? Are sick people helping other sick people? Many people do not know they are sick. You have seen the type.

For example: You have a problem with keeping your hands to yourself and another brother confides in you that he is struggling with the same thing. Instead of referring the person to someone who does not have the problem, you counsel him through your own pain. Two sick people trying to help each other. Now you have a big mess. You cannot help someone if you are sick yourself. Understand? Your stronghold is now

131

feeding another person's issue. Instead of being transparent before God and man, you would rather "fake the funk" and deceive the brethren.

Your stronghold is being projected onto someone else who needs help. Admittedly, you labored with the Lord; you reached out to God and asked for healing in your body, soul and spirit. This transformation and turning away from your old nature to the new nature has produced a strong witness for others. *Jeremiah 15:11 "The Lord said, Surely I will deliver you for a good purpose: surely I will make your enemies plead with you in times of disaster and times of distress."* Without deliverance, you pervert your witness. Believe that God will deliver you for a good purpose, but this will only happen if you are willing to go through the process of being changed into His image. Whatever purpose anyone else has placed in your mind, put it under your feet and move into the promises of God.

Rise up from your oppression and take back what the devil is trying to steal from you. The scripture states that you must stand firm, and do not let yourselves be burdened again by a yoke of slavery (*Galatians 5:1*). Being fearful of the unknown and unsure of what the future holds for you, can place a choke-hold on your life. God will never leave you or forsake you. God will complete the work He has anointed you to do. Reconciling yourself to the truth of where you are will reduce your desire to judge your spouse of his or her issues. All have fallen short of the glory of God. The Bible says to be careful not to judge others, because one day you could be judged by those same standards.

The trifling piece about judging is that it appears that the judge is exempt. But the person who considers himself or herself a judge will be held to a higher level of accountability. You will be held accountable for the words and deeds of your behavior. Before you want to chastise someone for his or her sin, be sure you are prepared to be chastised about your own indiscretions. At some point mercy and grace will be necessary for your trifling acts that have been brought to light.

Where did I go wrong?

David was extremely critical of other young people and their inability to stay celibate until marriage. David and Tina have one child named Christina. David made it his mission to straighten out other people's children in regards to sex. He did very little to show the love of God. He spent more time with other children then he did with his own child. David and Tina would ex-communicate couples and their families from the church because their child became pregnant out of wedlock. He made it a point to remove these individuals from all functions of the church.

David would condemn ministers who were unfaithful to their wives and call them out in church meeting. You can hear the other shoe dropping.... You know what happened next? David comes home to his own issue to handle. Christina is pregnant! David is devastated. He has no one to turn to and God does not appear to be hearing his cry for help. He puts his own daughter out of the house. In the meantime, David is developing a strategy to cover up his household's name. Tina is at her wits end. She is struggling to find out why this is happening to her family. What happened to all the petitions to God concerning her family? How did she fail God for such a punishment?

Christina's parents have forgotten what it is like to be young and immature. Everything is still centered on them. They have forgotten what it was like to be young and make mistakes. They forgot to pray for those who have fallen and then extend a hand of support before condemning someone. They forgot to show mercy and grace in order to build up the fallen while God walks them through their consequence. They forgot what love really looks like in the eyes of God.

Just a little talk with Jesús

David: Why have you forsaken me Jesus?

Jesus: I am right here with you David. Believe and don't doubt.

David: Where did I go wrong with my child? Christina has been going to church since she was born. How could she disgrace this family like this?

Jesus: I love you David even when you had that affair with the church secretary and she had an abortion remember?

David: That was different Lord. The secretary seduced me remember?

Jesus: All have sinned and need mercy and grace. The reaping and sowing process is in effect. I will be with you and never forsake you. Try extending this same love to your daughter.

David judged his daughter by the strongholds in his life. However the sins of the father were passed down to the child. Even though David's indiscretion was covered up, Christina's will be public in about three months. David forgot Christina's gifted voice. Her voice sounds like an angel from heaven. Regardless of her sin, her gift still resides within her. Her ability to usher the saints into the presence of God with her voice will not be diminished because she is pregnant. It is troubling that you lose your ability to show compassion to others when someone goes before God and the church asking forgiveness and the response is shame and silence. Now more than ever David and Tina will need to surround their daughter with love, compassion, understanding and long suffering. In the words of Jesus, "what you do to the least of these, you do unto me". (*Matthew 25:40*)

Judging someone by his or her strongholds is very easy to do. It takes the spotlight off your own mess. Stuff happens. Not to mention when you observe church folks who do not appear to be concerned that their behavior confuses the saints. Or they may know but do not care to change. You like being messy. This is not to say that people should not be held accountable for their actions. Pray that if the Lord leads you to speak life into another person's stronghold, that your approach will be in line with God. Mix humility, sprinkle gentleness and stand in the gap for each other as they work out their situations.

From a Trifling Act to a Treasured Response: Matthew 5:12

Seeking God's face results in forgiveness and healing. God will hear your humble pleas. He accepts your repentance and heals you where you hurt the most. When God extends mercy and grace in your direction, reciprocate this behavior to others. Each day you should ask God to forgive places where you have missed "the mark". Do unto others as you would have them do unto you. God is no respecter of person. In other words, if God will forgive anyone who asks forgiveness, you should be extending the same grace and mercy to others.

1. Do you concentrate on where others have failed and use their failure to justify your behavior?
2. In what areas in your marriage do you need to take a more forgiving approach?

Trifling Act Scene 22:
You can't hold water

Do you know why your spouse does not confide in you? Do you know why he or she can not open up and expose their innermost thoughts and insecurities? In the words of my mother, "you can't hold water". You struggle to hold on to sensitive information or to respect the information enough to value it as sacred. Your spouse is apprehensive to open up to you because he or she fears what you will do with the information. You have a reputation for sucker punching your spouse with sensitive information during the next strong disagreement or fight. No one wants their information broadcasted to the common man or woman. NO ONE!

It only takes one time for you to fail to be quiet about sensitive information. You are capable of maintaining your spouse's confidence. God has never commanded you to do anything that He feels you are incapable of doing. Jesus ate, walked, worked, worshipped and slept among the disciples for approximately three years. *John 13:18-30.* Yet every last one of them failed Him at the cross. Jesus spent a great deal of time exposing His character and purpose while on earth. However, the disciples could not handle or hold on to what Jesus would have to walk through.

Loose lips, sink ships.

Timothy and Michelle are having problems with their finances, their sex life and with their in-laws. The three big killers of a marriage are money, sex and family.

Timothy: I cannot believe that you told your mother what is going on in this house! We have enough problems.

Michelle: I do not know what you are talking about. Besides I really need someone to talk to just like you do.

Timothy: You know that you told your mother about our bedroom issues. Your mother asked me if I wanted to use some of your father's Viagra!

Michelle: I just told her that I did not feel loved. She asked me if I was withholding sex from you and I told her no! I needed to feel like I was still a woman. That's all.

Timothy: Don't you see that now you have embarrassed me and that I will not be able to look her in the face? Not to mention, you know she can't keep anything to herself. Remember that issue we had with our finances a few years ago? Your mother took up an offering for us at the church. I can't believe you would do this to us again.

Michelle: In my frustration, I blurted it out. I am really sorry.

Michelle has broken the golden rule. Never disclose sensitive information without verifying the individual has shown to be trustworthy. Remember everyone has

138

a close friend. Just as important, be careful when disclosing family information to relatives that have the same confidentiality issues you do. Additionally, do not discuss information with someone who does not love and support your spouse to the degree that he or she will challenge your mindset. Individuals that you confide in should be able to accept you and challenge your spiritual maturity, yet, still love you while you work out your issues. Let's take a look at another discussion.

Don't make me choose

Mother: Baby what is going on you sound upset.

Michelle: I am just frustrated with Tim. I do not feel loved and he is never interested in making love to me anymore.

Mother: Are you two fighting again? I told you Tim was not right for you. He doesn't even go to church half the time. You deserve better.

Michelle: Mom, please. I want our relationship to work. I don't want to leave him. I have bought out Victoria's Secret and it doesn't mean a thing to him. Not to mention the fact he won't go to the doctor to see if there is something wrong.

Mother: Baby, he must be having an affair.

Michelle: I've got to go now Mom. You are not helping the situation.

"Oh the tangled web we weave when first we practice to deceive." This conversation at best increased the frustration of the situation. Ladies, do not be ignorant of the devil's devices. You have been tricked into thinking that if you release your concerns to someone who cares about you that things will change. No! If you are not careful to whom you divulge your heart, you pervert the very situation you are struggling to resolve. There are several degrees of separation within a relationship. The marriage bed is definitely one of them.

When you look a little closer to Tim and Michelle's situation, there lays a root of betrayal that has penetrated the core of their relationship. Tim feels betrayed that his troubled manhood has been exposed. Michelle feels betrayed because her original ability to use sex as a way to penalize her husband has translated to Tim no longer caring to touch her. This is not to say that you should not seek sound counsel.....but be sure that the people you are confiding in are sound in the first place. Likewise be sure that the voice the counselor hears is that of God before he or she breathes life into your spirit.

Your spouse should live in an environment where he or she can be naked and un-ashamed. Men need to be respected and women need to be protected. Many times your spouse takes the information and files it under "blackmail" for a future date. Then you wonder why your spouse will not let his guard down and be real with you. How can this atmosphere continue when you call yourself a Christian? The answer is, it can't continue. This is why the divorce rate in the church is just as high as the divorce rate in the world. When you sit across a table with the knowledge that someone at the table will and has betrayed you, where do you go? Turn to Jesus as your example.

Can you imagine if you were Jesus sitting at the table breaking bread with Judas who would betray him with a kiss? This was a personal act of deception. *John 13:18* He who shares my bread....Breaking bread was a mark of close fellowship and those who brake bread with you hold a place of honor within your close circle. Jesus is your example of how you can have someone closer than close to you and yet know he or she cannot be trusted.

There are times when you feel like you are sleeping with the enemy. Acts that seem to kick you right in the chest and take your breath away are difficult for a spouse to manage in the flesh. Yet in John 13:19, Jesus reminds Himself that He continued to serve in order to reveal who God is. Jesus held His peace in order to fulfill the will of God. How about you? Are you willing to forgo speaking out of turn about your spouse in order to allow time to address the issue? Through the power of God's Word, learn to discuss differences without condemning each other. Learn how to make decisions without destroying unity. Decide to make it your purpose to give constructive suggestions without being demanding.

Choose to see your spouse differently today! Express an act of love that is designed for the other person's benefit or pleasure. This expression of love is simply a choice to be obedient. It is simple, when your motives and actions focus on how Jesus would love and give. Jesus started His day off praying. He drew strength from his Father first before extending Himself to others. He gave us a powerful example of how to fortify yourself before you interact with anyone.

From a Trifling Act to a Treasured Response: Matthew 6:9-13

1. What does your prayer life look like?
2. Does your prayer life include time praying as a couple?

One of the most intimate acts a couple can perform is praying for one another. Hearing your wife or husband open their heart and mind through prayer softens flesh and encourages the soul. Expressing compassion and love as God loves us through prayer is an intimate affair. There is nothing more powerful than to hear your husband pray for your hurting heart and wounded physical body. Take time to pray with one another. Praying over your food does not count.

Make a goal to take thirty minutes before you go to bed with each other and discuss what matters to each of you.

Discuss issues or praise reports that relate to each of you personally. During this thirty minute couple-time, resist the temptation to talk about the children, your money or your work. You will be amazed by the increased level of intimacy you will experience when you focus on each other.

Trifling Act Scene 23: Feel my pain

Can you walk in my shoes for just a day to grasp the sheer magnitude of my life? Can you comprehend the significance of working, cooking and cleaning only to be taken for granted by those who say they love you? Can someone please tell me why my family does not get it? The sheer desperation of the above questions prompts you to jump up and shout, "What is the deal?" Strange that you can live and eat with folks that are your flesh and blood, yet those same family members ignore the pain in your eyes.

It is possible to be in the middle of a crowded room and still feel lonely. This is not the military. The don't ask, don't tell philosophy does not work when you are attempting to build a relationship. Ignoring the obvious seems to be a habit that started in the Garden of Eden. Adam never asked where the fruit came from. Eve didn't ask the snake why he was talking to her instead of Adam. Why didn't anyone realize there was something wrong with this picture? Can it be that Adam was too busy counting the animals to see his wife was hanging out with the wrong crowd?

The Eves of this world are feeling the curse of eating the fruit in the Garden of Eden. Her curse was to bare pain in labor. Since the incident in the garden, women have exhibited greater emotions regarding their circumstances compared to men. To contemplate the level of pain and disappointment Eve endured after exiting the only home she knew; imagine the feeling of spiritual separation Adam experienced when he no longer felt the presence of God.

You do have to admire Eve for her faith in God's Word, regardless of how distorted that faith was. She took God at His Word. Her child would crush the head of the very enemy that assisted in her expulsion from the Garden of Eden. Along comes baby Cain. Eve was saying, "I feel vindicated." Adam on the other hand is still wondering why Eve is 'tripping'. The only reference about Adam after the eviction was Adam "knew" his wife, in the Biblical sense. There is a consistent struggle for a man to understand the emotional whirlpool that a woman can and will go through at any time. A woman wants a man to "feel her pain"!

Allow me to use myself as an example. Twenty five years ago in order to get a marriage license I was required to take a blood test. I told Darryl that I was petrified of needles. Being the man he is, Darryl said, no problem. He committed to going with me so that we could get our tests together. "No biggie." Those were his words exactly. We got to the doctor's office. The nurse states that the doctor will call me back in about 15 minutes. By the time the nurse called my name I am in a cold sweat. Do you think Darryl realized it? Nope. Why? Because for 15 minutes I told him stuff like, "I am feeling really sick. I don't think I can do this. I really have to go lay down." During all of these statements, Darryl was reading a magazine and did not make any eye contact. Until the nurse called my name and I was as pale as a white sheet! Needless to say, the nurse barely got enough blood for the test. After this incident, Darryl paid closer attention to me when

144

needles are involved. I was attempting to connect with Darryl by exposing a weakness I had with needles.

In short, connecting with your spouse during rough times can bring you closer or drive you apart. Usually the reason why the husband can not accept the wife's emotional outburst is because he does not know where he stands as it relates to the problem. The question is "Honey I need to know are you upset with me or upset about something else?" To ask this question will expose the husband to a woman who may expect him to already know the answer! The husband walks right into a trap he cannot escape from. Wake up wives! Your husbands are not mind readers nor can they perform the Vulcan mind melt that Spock used on the Starship Enterprise. Men need tangible and factual information to decipher whether they will sleep on the couch or in the bed next to you. On the other hand, a woman wants to know if she is the most important person in the world to you next to God. When you demonstrate this act of kindness and concern, your mate will embrace just about anything. Why, because you have already proven what is important.

When your spouse does not feel your pain, you find yourself acting in a manner that will force your spouse to feel your distress. Please do not take this approach. It will only cause your husband to withdraw and become confused. Another method you may utilize is speaking the Word of God inappropriately to justify your behavior. Taking scripture out of context in order to condemn your spouse because he or she fails to meet your needs is not Godly.

Can't we get along?

Beverly and Todd are at odds with each other because Beverly will not submit when it comes to paying bills. Beverly grew up sacrificing. She feels it is her turn to live a good life that her pocket book cannot afford. Because their arguments continue to center on her inability to manage her spending, they are not addressing the real issue at hand. Like many issues that exist in a relationship it is necessary to take a look at your own behavior before you determine that your spouse does not understand you. Yet, when taking a retrospective analysis of your situation, you may still fail to identify the culprit behind the problem. Translation: "You say I have a problem, but I don't see it!" Therefore you cause pain in strategic places to produce a profound reaction.

Is it really necessary?

Todd is a loving husband and gives Beverly the world as it relates to loving and living. He has however, made some consistent undertones that her spending habits are really starting to affect their financial security. Beverly decides she needs a "girl's day-out" with Gwen. Beverly and Gwen leave the department store on their way to the restaurant for dinner. Beverly has her hands full of shopping bags. Impulse buying feeds her control issues.

Beverly: I really needed this shopping trip.
Gwen: Girl, you have plenty of clothes and shoes. You do not need one other thing.
Beverly: Now you are sounding like Todd. I need a release and shopping does that for me.

146

Gwen: Hey don't shoot the messenger! You told me to be your sanity check as it relates to spending. Remember the budget you're on? Remember the last intense conversation you and Todd had last week?

Beverly: I know, I know. Hey can you put these shopping bags in your trunk?

Gwen: I will not...that is straight trifling. Either take the bags in the house or take the bags back to the department store? Your choice.

Beverly: Ok, Ok, after dinner, please take me back to the store. But I am keeping the shoes!

Gwen: You don't need another pair of shoes. You will not hide those shoes from Todd in my trunk.

At some point, Beverly will need to feel a little pain in order to understand the impact of her spending habits on her family. Additionally, it would not be a bad idea for Beverly to educate herself on money management and the impact of emotional spending. Beverly may need to go on a fast that eliminates all personal shopping while God works with her desire to feed her own desires. A suggestion for Beverly would be to establish a covenant with her husband which outlines how she will correct her need to spend.

From a Trifling Act to a Treasured Response: Matthew 17:21

Fast and pray and live holy everyday. Your desires should line up with the will of God. Fasting and praying to God about your areas of opportunity can and will break the problems in your life. True fasting will bring your flesh under submission and prompt the spirit to move on your behavior. There are some pains that are difficult to release without the empowering of the Holy Spirit. Nor can you call on God when you do not believe. Jesus said the disciples had little faith. He acknowledges that His disciples at least believed to a point. How about you? Do you have the faith to see your marriage improve?

Ask God to place an accountability partner into your life. An accountability partner is a praying friend who stands in the gap for you. He or she will challenge the way you see the situation. He or she can be your prayer warrior interceding on your behalf in and out of the seasons of your life.

Trifling Act Scene 24:
I have a headache

C an someone tell me what a headache has to do with making love to your husband? When you want something from one another you make a sacrificial offering of love. Before you got married, all you could think about was the "booty call" event. Now that you are married and free to please one another on a regular basis without guilt; your sexual appetite seems to be tied up with a headache. You did not have a headache before you got married! Trust me, the mistress that he may have on the side is not telling him she has a headache. Flesh issues are dominating couples who are preparing for marriage. Many couples in the church are openly living together before they get married. Most of them say it is because they are saving money for their wedding. Some justify their living arrangements by rationalizing it is convenient or that they know they are getting married in few months.

Sex before marriage distorts your view of each other. Yet you get married, sex is guilt free and now everything is locked up tighter than a chastity belt. You're finally free to love without limitation. Here is how this works; men **NEED** sex to feel loved. Women **GIVE** sex to feel loved. *Hebrews 13:4* talks about keeping the marriage bed honorable. When the flesh steps outside of the obedience of God, adultery is one of the results. An honorable marriage bed prevents the devil from invading the blessings of God. Many people

149

can't handle this divine revelation. If you believed in honoring your bedroom, you would only minister in a physical and emotional way to your own spouse. Inviting someone other than your spouse into your bed is an act of selfish disobedience to God.

Anytime you go to a selfish state of mind your behavior will begin to smell. Fish that is left out on the kitchen table for more than a day will stink. Your foul attitude will contaminate your relationship. Do you love God more than allowing your flesh to have its way? Selfish attitudes allow you to focus on your job more than your relationship. You will spend more time hanging out with your home boys instead of your "boring wife". Every married man has heard the "I have a headache, I don't feel well, and I'm not sure what's wrong with me today." Usually a few things have happened to cause this disconnect to occur in a relationship. The wife is mad at the husband for some legitimate or illegitimate reason. Ladies, the fact is a man can be mad as a hornet and still want to make love to you.

Oh, but hubby watch out when your wife is hurt and upset. The love shop is on lock down and the husband is not getting any loving tonight. Her statements are: "Don't touch me, don't talk to me and your breath stinks!" Women have to feel loved to make love to their husbands. My husband tries to tell other men that women are emotionally connected to the image of relationships. That is why soap operas exist today. Anyway, husbands if you want to make love to your wife start in the morning. Call her; arrange to have dinner ready when she comes home; take care of those bad kids of yours so that she feels that she has energy to take care of you later.

Wives when you do not take care of your man in the bedroom you are encouraging him to wander someplace you don't want him to go. Those individuals, who have strongholds in the area of sex, often struggle to manage the urge to step out on the wild side. Even those that profess Christianity will surprise their pastor with the confession of infidelity. The good news is where there is knowledge there is power.

Jesus is the Lamb of God who takes away the sin of the world. When Jesus died on the cross, every sin known to man was nailed to that cross. Be firmly persuaded that God has forgiven you. Know that when you repent and ask for forgiveness, God is faithful to extend mercy and grace to those who move in the direction of obedience. God called the husband and the wife to love one another. Do not confuse loving one another with accepting poor behavior or character flaws that require correction. Withholding sex is dishonorable and destructive to a relationship. Manipulation will not produce a permanent behavior change in your spouse; it is a selfish act.

If a past hurt is causing you to withdraw from your spouse then go to God and ask Him to remove the hurt and replace it with His peace. This sensitive area is a direct target for the devil. It is important for you to recognize and guard your sex area as close as possible. Once you have prayed for divine revelation, move with extreme prejudice to a resolution. Place a hedge of protection around your intimacy zones by having open and honest conversations with your spouse about your needs and wants. Then, talk about sexual fulfillment, boundaries, limitations and expectations pertaining to performance and expressing intimacy to each other.

151

Communicate verbally before communicating physically. Make love to your spouse in words before you touch him or her with your hands. Ask your spouse to forgive you for playing mind games. One of those mind games is having sex with your spouse to get something that was not in the budget. You have managed to "prostitute" your way into getting what you want from your spouse. A prostitute performs an act for an individual for a price. In the same way, you want a new dress. You become extra nice to your spouse in order to get your way. A husband will make sure all the kids are bathed and dinner prepared so that he can get busy with his wife that night. This act of support is rarely exhibited except when he wants loving from his wife. Little does he know that she has figured out his scheme and feels he has reduced her to a piece of meat. Any other time, he does not lift a finger to help her around the house. In other words, you start turning tricks in order to get what you want from your mate. Sometimes it works and sometimes you don't have enough money to pay the tab you are racking up!

Manipulation does not equate to love. It shows a lack of respect and honor toward your spouse. Love is patient and kind. It does not boast and does not keep record of wrongs. Love does not seek its own. Manipulation is the exact opposite of loving someone like Christ loved the church.

From a Trifling Act to a Treasured Response: Matthew 5:6

"Blessed are they which do hunger and thirst after righteousness: for they shall be filled."

Be careful what you feed your temple. There are some things that your friend may tolerate that God will not allow you to touch. You may not have the spiritual maturity to deal with the temptation. Corruption is difficult to combat when the individual does not want to let go of the sin that so easily has engulfed them. The Holy Spirit convicts you of your inappropriate behavior. The conviction should lead to change not denial. You are the physical witness on earth of the spirit intercessor, Jesus, in heaven. Do not allow your witness to be tarnished by a carnal act of disobedience. Get to a place spiritually, where it is your daily mission to obey God in all things.

1. Establish a regular Bible study with your spouse. This exercise is intended to produce understanding. Do not make studying the Bible a debate with your spouse.
2. Keep a journal for 30 days that is dedicated to your spouse. In the journal write every significant discussion and the impact of the discussion. After the first 30 days, compare what you thought was significant compared to your spouse. Make an effort to recognize what is important to your spouse.

Trifling Act Scene 25:
I smell smoke

L ife is really worth living, not worth going up in smoke. The life of a modern day couple is fast and furious. The schedules of most school age children can out-perform the average corporate account executive. Add your personal "to do" list with your children's basketball, football and Brownie schedule and you have the makings of a three-alarm fire. The pre-occupation with being all you can be has today's couple burning themselves out at both ends. "Having it all" and "Doing it all" is burning up relationships with a focus on momentum moving events instead of quality communication.

Take a look at the following list of smoke burning events:

- You are saved and you know you are saved, yet you marry someone tall, tan and unsaved. It is a known fact that individuals who are unequally yoked, struggle spiritually and emotionally. There is something to be said about studying and observing your mate before you marry him or her. Do not settle for less than God's best. Even if that means waiting on His divine timing instead of yours. Those of you who have stepped out on faith and believe God for a miracle remember your witness will cause restoration to your spouse.

- An aggressive wife makes all the decisions because the head of the house is too busy working, to spend time at home. Without a strong head, the rest of the body does not know how to move properly or effectively. Something will be burning in the kitchen and it will be more than his wife's bra. When the proper covering does not exist in the house, decisions are made without the benefit of information from your husband. This scene is frustrating for both the husband and the wife. The husband stands on his bread winning position and the wife defends her necessity to call the shots position. All the while the family is dysfunctional.

- More money is flowing out of the house and you are passing blame instead of taking accountability. You ask, take responsibility for what? It is called a budget! Get one and stick to it. Make the decision to sacrifice. Yes, budget is a hard word to comprehend in a world that has to have everything now, but obedience is better. The ability to be a good steward of what God has given you exemplifies obedience. Additionally, make an agreement with each other regarding what and how you spend money. When Darryl and I were in dire straits we agreed to call each other if either of us wanted to spend more than $50.00. Pay your bills together. Everyone will be on the same page when it comes to knowing what is left in the checking account.

- Stop ignoring each other to prevent an argument. Do not let the sun go down on your wrath. Ignoring an issue which is important to the security of your relationship will only result in magnifying the problem. Silence is a form of agreement. Saying nothing actually implies that you are cool with how the discussion progressed. Silence does not result in resolution just frustration. The concept of returning to your separate corners is only effective in boxing matches not in life or love. Besides, the good book says if you love someone, you are long suffering, kind and do not hold grudges or meditate on wrong actions. If you need time to re-group, agree on the amount of time and then reconcile with each other.

- Taking responsibility for adult children instead of challenging grown folks to manage themselves. Grown people do grown things. Parents can encourage and provide advice without providing financial support. A man should not eat if he cannot take care of his family. You are not responsible for taking care of your son's family or your daughter's family. If they are up to their eyeballs in debt, and their spending habits have not improved, you are enabling them by throwing money their way. Of course if the basic needs of life are in jeopardy, God would expect you to have compassion. At some point, everyone needs a helping hand. Just be sure you have not established a pattern which results in a handout.

- Taking care of a career, home and husband. Losing self and losing ground spiritually in the process. You have lost your balance. Make a schedule that incorporates "me" time. When you give out more without replenishing yourself physically and spiritually, resentment and fatigue ensues. You have made the decision to have it all. Have you asked God if your current lifestyle is permanent or temporary? Line your life up with your purpose and rest in knowing that each day your efforts move you closer to God and His mission.

Smoke and broken glass can be seen and heard everywhere in all of the above examples. Focus people, focus! Activities that cloud and distort your God-given vision are weapons used by Satan.

It should not be this hard

Melinda: I had no idea that marriage would be this hard. I can't even breathe without getting interrogated. It is easier to run an executive board meeting than to figure out my husband.

Alicia: As your spiritual advisor, what did you expect of your husband? You are still in the honeymoon stages of your marriage.

Melinda: I am used to going and coming the way I used to. Now I have to check in with Chris. Not to mention the fact that this whole budget thing is really overrated.

Alicia: Sounds like you still have a "single life" mentality. You are married! You mentioned that it is easier to run a meeting than to figure out your husband. Tell me what you do to prepare for a meeting.

Melinda: I have a whole check list of things to do. As a project manager, I am responsible for understanding how the product works and how to best present the benefits of the product. Many times I will spend a good month researching the product.

Alicia: How much time are you going to spend studying and researching Chris? What are his strengths and his weaknesses? How does he spell love or honor? The same effort you put into being a success in business can be used to be a success in your marriage.

Melinda: The people at work listen to me. Chris challenges my spending habits and everything.

Alicia: That is his job to challenge your thinking. The Lord joined the two of you together for a reason. Chris and his responsible attitude is the very thing you fell in love with. God gave you what you wanted and what you needed. Don't let the devil take your focus off of your blessing and your goal for a successful marriage.

Marriage does take work. It can be rewarding or it can be a struggle to justify your reason for waking up every morning. The devil is a cunning creature. Satan will encourage a smoke filled environment to deceive and confuse the life of the believer. When a couple does not work as one, they produce a cloud which affects the living organism called marriage. The goal of all couples should be to live as one effective force for the Kingdom of God. Take hold of all incomplete areas in the relationship before the smoke consumes you both. Where there is smoke, fire is on the tail end of your situation. Smoke is a warning sign that something demands attention and redirection. Find the fire extinguisher and handle your business before the devil gets an entire foot-hold. Your goal should be to fire proof your relationship.

From a Trifling Act to a Treasured Response: Proverbs 4:25

What is your action plan? What is your strategy for improving your relationship? When was the last time you discussed your vision with your spouse? These are all questions that set your marriage on the right path. Couples who take an active role in evaluating and searching for ways to serve each other better are more fulfilled in their relationships.

1. Study your spouse. Be the expert as it relates to what your spouse likes and dislikes.

2. Identify what motivates or devalues your mate.

3. Carefully pray and consider how God would have you lift up your spouse.
4. Write a vision statement for your family.

Trifling Act Scene 26: I'm not feeling it!

Whenever you ask my father how he is feeling, the reply is usually, "I feel with my hands!" His philosophy is how a person feels should have nothing to do with how a person behaves. Go ahead and feel with your hands, but think with your head and move with your heart. On average people are only aware of 20% of their thoughts, feelings, and motives. Once I read in a magazine that we repeat negative thoughts 600 times a day. No wonder you have no feelings, everything is numb from the neck down.

Take possession of your thought process through the Word of God. Remind yourself who and whose you are- you are a child of the living God. You are an heir to the throne with power to overcome those things that could overtake you. *Psalms 8: 4-8* speaks of how you are made a little lower than angels and crowned with glory and honor. Jesus said, "I have given you authority to trample..." When you feel bound, broke, and defeated by the stresses of life, God's Word reminds you to rise up and trample on your situations.

When the snakes of life come your way- ungrateful bosses, people who lack integrity, and flirtatious people in the church - put God's Word on the situation. When the scorpion sting of discouraging words that wound, or an unfaithful husband or disappointing children come against your spirit, put the Word on it. Use God's

163

Word like a set of keys. The keys to your car can make a V8 engine pay attention. Take the keys of faith and run over those situations with God's powerful Words of truth and love. His Word alone can move your spirit into an empowering state of grace. "Nothing will harm you". Jesus knew that believing in the power of God would place your name in heaven. God will send a Word your way to strengthen your spirit, and you can shout "I think I can, I think I can!"

The covenant of Sarah and Abraham

This brings me to one of my favorite spiritual women, Sarah. Let's use Sarah, Abraham's wife, as an example of a sister who rose up from the oppressions of life. A woman who was not feeling the fact that God indeed would open her womb and birth a child in her old age. Everyone knows Sarah. Sarah was Abraham's wife, who never had a child until divine intervention occurred. God always fulfills His promises. She becomes the mother of Isaac. Through Isaac, she became the grandmother of Jacob, who God later renamed Israel. Sarah is one of the ancestors of all the Israelites and of Jesus Christ. In *Genesis 17:15-16*, God told Sarah that she would be blessed with a son. Sarah would be the mother of nations and Kings of people will come from her. Abraham and Sarah as husband and wife both shared in the covenant promises of God.

Yet, Sarah allowed her own doubts of having a child to oppress her purpose. How could a woman at the age of 90 have a child? Her negative thoughts consumed her on a regular basis. She took no solace in the fact

164

that even at her mature age Pharaoh and Abimelech wanted her. This woman had it going on. She took into account Abraham's age of 100 and knew for sure that the equipment had rusted and the factory wasn't working anymore. In *Genesis 18:12 Sarah laughed to herself as she thought, after I am worn out and my master is old, will I now have this pleasure*? Sarah was saying, "I couldn't even have fun trying to have a baby!"

How many of you are laughing at the potential God has in store for you? How many of you believe there is no way you will be happy in your marriage? How many of you have cried tears of frustration and aggravation because your womb is hollow with disappointments? But God....chimes in on Sarah, "Is anything too hard for the Lord?" Take hold of the covenant promises between Abraham, Sarah and God. Allow your womb to jump with possibilities.

Can you recover from a storm?

Three months have lapsed since the betrayal occurred. Henry felt pretty safe that his wife would never find out he really failed the family. He was virtually in the clear. Yet, each Sunday, his conscience would get the best of him. He really loved his wife and knew he made a big mistake cheating on Cyndi.

Henry: Cyndi, there is something I need to tell you.
Cyndi: Ok, I am all ears.
Henry: What would you say if I told you I had an affair?

Cyndi: What kind of question is that? I would be very disappointed and extremely hurt. But I would forgive you.

Henry: Would you forgive the other woman as well, even if the affair is over? You know, just a hypothetical question?

Cyndi is looking intently into Henry's eyes. It is clear that Henry is not speaking about a random person. Her heart seemed to drop to the bottom of her shoes. He really did have an affair! Her head is reeling and searching for visible signs of betrayal. Yet, she loves him and believes in the covenant of marriage.

Cyndi: (nervous response) Then why tell the wife if the affair is over? Are you feeling guilty Henry?

Henry: I didn't have an affair. However, I did spend our entire life savings at the casino. I had no idea that I had such a problem.

Cyndi knew that money was systematically missing from the checking account. However, she could not put her finger on where the money was going. Then there were times where extra money would show up in the account, but Henry always had an answer.

Cyndi: What are we going to do? Will we lose the house? How could you do this to the family? This is worse than you cheating on me. You failed our family, our future.

Henry: I am confessing to you because it is the right thing to do and I want to be right with both you and God. Will you forgive me?

Cyndi: You think pleading forgiveness will get you off the hook. You will reap what you sow. I can hardly look at you, yet alone forgive you. At least if you had an affair the problem would go away. Now we have to start all over.

Henry and Cyndi are between a rock and a hard place called debt. It is an example of how the decisions of one person can impact the life of others. Henry thought that if he gave a situation of infidelity to Cyndi that finding out about the money would be a relief for her. He did not count on Cyndi condemning herself for failing to open her mouth about the inconsistent cash flow. She was angry that she had ignored her discerning spirit. Henry filtered out over $100,000 over a period of nine months. Their entire life savings was gambled away. Henry failed to understand that there are many ways to be unfaithful in your marriage. Trust is a characteristic that must be earned. Cyndi must be willing to trust herself and her husband again. The love she has for Jesus must sustain her broken heart. Could your marriage stand the storm?

From a Trifling Act to a Treasured Response: Hebrews 11:11

By Faith even Sarah herself, when she was barren, received power to conceive offspring even though she was past the age, since she considered that the One who had promised was faithful.

When you are faithless, God is faithful. He is not a man who can lie. Sarah trusted Abraham though he lied about their relationship with others. The lies placed her in a position that could have nullified the plan and purpose God had for Sarah to be the mother of many nations. Sarah had great faith and respect in Abraham. She assumed innocence. The assumption was that Abraham would never do anything that would put her in harms way. Abraham did not see the precious gift God placed within his wife. Imagine if Sarah did not trust Abraham.

Many of you do not trust your husband or wife. Trust is difficult to regain when lost. The person that cannot be trusted would appreciate a second chance. The person who has lost confidence in their spouse refuses to expose his or her heart to another potential injury. Trust that God will take care of you. Trust God to heal your spouse as you step out on faith to believe; change and trust again. Take steps to see the faithfulness of God in your life and the commitment your spouse has made to change. God will help you move from responding from a hurting position to a healing position as your spouse works toward reconciliation.

Trifling Act Scene 27:
Secrets saved for marriage

There are some things that you really should find out about your spouse **before** you get married. This is why pre-marital counseling is so important. Do any of the following situations sound familiar? It is not good to find out after you get married that the reason why your wife is frigid in the bed is due to her father molesting her at a young age. Learning that your husband does not want children and you want a house full of them is not good. Finding out that your husband was married before he married you and never got an official divorce decree, *really* is not good. Learning that your wife has an addiction to spending and you believe that recycling is cutting off the sweat stained sleeves of your old tee shirt to make it a workout shirt, is not good. It is so embarrassing that your friends offer to chip in to buy an actual workout shirt, and then you use it as a car shammy! These are secrets that should not be saved until after you get married.

Secrets are the ingredients that divorces are made of in this day and time. Stated previously, money, sex and family are three areas that every couple should discuss extensively before they get married. If there are skeletons in a person's closet, the bones will be found in the areas of money, sex and family. The big three killers of a marriage are alive and well.

You have heard the saying of the three things that you better not mess with- My woman/man, my food and my money. So why in the world would you omit discussing these critical topics with your soon-to-be mate? Why not? The fear of rejection is more than you can bear to handle. The fear of losing a man or woman that you know is your soul mate will prompt you to turn and look the other way regarding important issues.

As Darryl and I sit on the other side of an engaged couple and we bring up the subject of the 'big' three killers of a marriage, it never fails to amaze us when the couples state that these issues are under control.

Conversations regarding how they are going to handle their finances and establish a joint budget are all under control. The couple will figure it out after they get married- so they think! Looks like a sign of denial. Working out money issues will reveal how well a couple can communicate through adversity. Both of you should get a copy of your credit report and list all outstanding obligations. If you can work through a budget you are going a long way to effectively communicating your position regarding marriage as it relates to money. It's been said that the average individual carried 12 credit cards in his/her pocket. That's 12 opportunities for a couple to be saddled with long term unsecured debt. Know your audience and how they spell relief. If relief to them is spelled – S H O P P I N G, then you have some serious discussing to do.

It's a family affair

Family is the next big hurdle. How do you address the overly possessive mother who refuses to let go. You

170

realized you had a problem when you and the groom to be were planning the details for the wedding and the mother of the groom goes on and on about how she wants this and she wants that. Meanwhile, the groom has his head in his hand without speaking a word. Your folks on the other hand are fit to be tied because all your cousins want to come to the $125 per person sit down dinner. The wedding is financed by both the bride and groom. You have no intentions of spending money on people you do not like. Details, details...all of which require a solid plan of action by the couple before others regulate your destiny. Will you allow your family to rule and rain on your parade or will you take a stand and establish your own traditions? For this reason, a man shall leave his father and mother and cleave to his wife.

Sexual Freedom

Sex is the next hot topic. You would think that this would be the easiest topic for an engaged couple. Not so! The dynamics of how society perceives sex has infiltrated the Christian mindset as well. Many couples have had previous sexual experiences before taking their vows. As a matter of fact there are Christian couples who believe cohabitation is acceptable. They have all kinds of rationale about their position. None of them are in line with the Word of God and being obedient.

For example: "We need to save money for the wedding. So living together is cost effective."

"We have already planned the wedding. It is just a matter of time before the marriage will be official."

171

"Please, why would I deprive my fiancé of pleasure when I know we are going to be married soon?"

The problem is that once you have physically connected with someone, you lose your sense of objectivity. Sex before marriage distorts something that God intended to be a special loving event for a married couple. The issues which would cause you to be sensitive to a potential problem will be overlooked and discarded because that is what sex does to you. It will blind you to the truth. I call it, "Blinded by the Booty!" The scripture talks about shunning from the pure appearance of evil. (*2 Thessalonians 5:22*) Heavy physical foreplay will get you into other acts of intimacy that can put you in a state of no return...if you know what I mean.

People, is it important for you to know who you are sleeping with before you go to bed with them. Consider Leah and Jacob. (*Genesis 29:16*) Jacob was required to work seven years for Rachel, the younger sister. However, after the wedding night, he awoke the next morning to Leah, the older sister sleeping next to him. If only Jacob had looked under the covers before performing his consummation, seven extra years of hard work and grief could have been avoided.

You need to know what you're getting into. Look beyond the physical aspects of an individual and identify what he or she thinks, believes, and feels are important. Are they trying to be a man or woman of God? What goals have they established for themselves? Do their priorities line up correctly? Your priorities will determine the level of support you will get later in your relationship. A man only wants his woman to be about him alone. The challenge with this concept is that he will work to change her. All of a sudden now he understands that submission means she has do to what he says. However, submission is aligning your goals and aspirations according to God and with each other in mind.

Rule number # 1 of marriage
You cannot change a person.

Rule number # 2 of marriage
A person will change when he or she wants to change.

The question you must ask yourself is this: If he/she never changes can I live and love them as they are?

Demanding that your spouse be responsible for your joy or lack thereof is trifling and you know it. Unfortunately, no one person can fulfill all your needs alone. If one person could fulfill your needs, why would you need or depend on the Lord to sustain you?

When I state that no one person can fulfill your needs I am not insinuating that you should have a mistress or dude on the side. What I am saying is that there is no way that one person can be everything, at every time, in every situation for you.

Deuteronomy 30:19-20 talks about God giving us a choice between life and death. In the conversation, the Lord even gives you the answer. You are to choose life. Choosing life has its benefits in the eyes of the Lord. Choosing life will allow your children and yourself to live long. However, the Word is clear; you must listen for His voice and hold fast to what God has said in His

Word. It is the only way to get clarity and direction that will never fail.

From a Trifling Act to a Treasured Response: Hebrew 3:7

The Holy Spirit speaks. Are you listening? The Holy Spirit gives direction. Are you walking in the new light of understanding? You have moved from listening from a carnal perspective to one that is spirit led. Are you willing to be naked and unashamed before God, to move from faithlessness to faithfulness? The Holy Spirit will tell you to go home instead of taking a few drinks with the guys. The Holy Spirit will tell you to hold your peace instead of disrespecting your husband when he begs forgiveness. The beautiful fact is that you are accepted through the blood of Jesus Christ. The Holy Spirit within you is the witness that God is completing His work in you.

Trifling Act Scene 28:
He's my Cave Man!

O ne of the most challenging things a counselor will encounter is having to advise a couple that the road ahead of them is going to be an emotional and spiritual endeavor. Darryl and I will never tell a couple they should not get married. That is not our responsibility. Our responsibility is to bring up the issues that the Lord has laid on our hearts and communicate the information with love to the couple. One such couple that sticks out in my mind was Jennifer and Nathan. In an effort to be obedient to the covenant of marriage and God, they decided it was time to get married. This couple already had one child out of wedlock. The wedding plans were set. The church was notified and reserved. The pastor could perform the wedding. The only thing left to do was to "check in" with the marriage ministry leaders two weeks before the wedding. Keep in mind that at this point, the counseling piece is just a formality for the couple - so they think.

I want to be free and married

Jennifer and Nathan were mature in age and understood the importance of God and covenant. There were several warning signs observed since the engagement where Jennifer just did not believe that Nathan was ready to settle down. Jennifer was younger than Nathan by a number of years. There was a definite age gap and mindset to contend with. Additionally, over the past four years of dating, living together and living apart Nathan learned to enjoy the freedom that comes with single living, yet he loves Jennifer with a passion.

During one of our counseling sessions, it appeared that Nathan was emphatic about keeping some of his single tendencies. For example, Nathan did not feel there was anything wrong with taking a 2-hour "man time" beer break after work before coming home. Jennifer on the other hand, was waiting with baited breath at the door for him to relieve her of their child. Nathan also enjoyed his "man time" breaks on weekends which were eating away at Jennifer emotionally. She felt Sunday should be family time only and hanging out with his home boys was not considered appropriate.

Man down- Man down

Nathan: I don't see anything wrong with hanging out with the boys. You never want me to do anything with the fellows.

Jennifer: That is not true. I just believe you should spend just as much time if not more with your family than you do with your single friends who do not support your marriage.

Nathan: Oh lighten up Jennifer. I make sure that I have checked in with you don't I?

Jennifer: Your idea of checking in is six hours after you have left and you promised you would be back in four hours. Then when I try to call you on the phone, you don't pick up.

Nathan: Yeap, because I know all you are going to do is make me feel guilty so that I would come home, but I was having fun.

Jennifer: Don't you see we, I mean I, want to spend time with you?

Nathan: I do spend time with you and the baby, on the weekends and on Sunday mornings.

Jennifer: Sunday mornings, but what about the whole day?

Nathan: The whole day! I need time for me too!

Jennifer: What!! You spend time with your 'boys' every other weekend and every Thursday and Friday night.

Nathan: That is not my time that is time with the fellows.

Jennifer: That's my Cave Man!

It is clear that the transition from singleness to married is going to be a journey filled with challenges. I told Jennifer to remember those words when Nathan does not conform to her ideal impression of a Godly husband. Not that Nathan cannot rise up from his oppression and be all the husband and father that God has called him to be. NO, that is not the point. The point is Jennifer and Nathan are walking into a relationship that already shows they are unequally yoked as it relates to their spiritual understanding of the Word and how to effectively apply it.

Given time and opportunity, this couple will experience one of two seasons. They will endure a long winter transition or sweet spring of revelations that transforms them into a more harmonious place of rest. It is always difficult to witness a couple struggling through issues that are definitely transparent to the naked eye. This is why getting physically connected with an individual before marriage is so damaging. It distorts the vision and damages your ability to see the true person within.

The one hundred dollar question had to be asked before we wished the couple well. If Jennifer or Nathan never changes can they live with each other for the rest of their lives? They said a resounding yes, and we left the table promising to attend the wedding.

Only God can change the heart of a man or woman. Jennifer is counting on the fact that once Nathan is married he will change. Don't count on it. The longer it takes for the average male or female to get married, the more set in his or her ways they become. Because of the strong resistance to bringing about change, the old habits Nathan exhibits will not change quickly or go quietly into the night. He has no intention of giving up his beer, late nights and fellows, without a fight. Jennifer has taken a position of religiosity! She has an understanding of the Word, yet lacks the application of the Word of God.

When the scripture speaks of loving your neighbor as yourself (*Matthew 19:19*), Jennifer will need to reconcile her understanding of submission with that of the Word and embrace the position she "willed" into her life, with God giving her strength to endure until Nathan 'gets it'. The strongest bond that Jennifer and Nathan have is their commitment to God and to each other, regardless of where that commitment will take them. In the end, the wedding was beautiful and the marriage is thriving.

From a Trifling Act to a Treasured Response: Philippians 4:7

Place your concerns and worries in the hands of God, the maker of peace. His peace is so great that it surpasses any form of relief imaginable. When you have peace about a decision, you know that God is in the middle of the decision. God is not a God of confusion. Seek His face, walk in His Word and believe that He is guarding your heart and mind through the blood of Jesus. Once you have your revelation walking papers from God, be a bold witness for Christ in your marriage. The time it took to get your spouse is the same amount of time it takes to keep her or him. Establish a regular date night. Renew your desire to spend time with each other over others. Life is too short to live life out of the will of God. Do something, get moving and stand firm in the power of God.

Trifling Act Scene 29:
Get behind the action

For every action there is a reaction. Each time you move in a direction is indicative of historical data accumulated regarding that subject. Translation: When your spouse forgets for the fifth time to take out the trash, you make a move. The action is that your spouse failed to honor something he or she said they would do. Historically, every Thursday, your husband will wait until the trash man has passed your house before running the receptacle to the curb. Therefore, you decide that placing the trash can behind his car, so that he moves it to the curb made sense to you. Until he ran over the trash can and put a dent in the car. The action was to get the trash can to the curb. The reaction is now a heated discussion about you treating your husband like a child that does not need to be told about his chores. Somewhere this couple has failed to determine what is motivating each other's actions.

Why is your wife acting crazy again tonight? Why does your husband stay out all night with the guys? Why don't we have sex more often? In order to get to the root of the problem, you must get beyond the behavior to determine the emotional motive associated with the action.

What is your motivation?

Jeremiah has had it up to his chin with Sydney complaining about how he is not meeting her needs. He works over 40 hours a week. He helps with the kids and around the house. Once a week he goes out with the guys for a few beers. Jeremiah believes that as a grown man, he can do what he wants to do, when he wants to do it. What is the harm with that? Why does Sydney have to be so critical of his friends?

Sydney: When are you going to be home tonight?

Jeremiah: I don't know. This is my night to have a good time. Must we go over this again?

Sydney: You drink too much and your friends are not interested in supporting this marriage.

Jeremiah: You are over-exaggerating the situation. You know good and well that I do not drink and drive. Now you are trying to pick a fight before I leave. But be clear woman, I am leaving to go out with the guys tonight!

Sydney: You seem more excited about going out with the guys than spending time with your own family. When was the last time you took me out?

Jeremiah: (Mumbling under his breath) Why would I take you anywhere? All you do is nag.

Sydney: I heard that. I hope you enjoy sleeping on the couch tonight.

Jeremiah: Oh Lord, here we go again.

Sydney: Don't put God in the middle of your mess. You are the one ignoring your responsibilities.

It does not appear that Jeremiah or Sydney is making progress regarding Jeremiah's entertainment options. From the dialogue it appears there is a deeper issue at hand that is being ignored. They are missing the motivation that is driving the behavior. When your focus is exclusively on the behavior, you will miss the significant problem that continues to rear its ugly head. Attack the situation and the motivation behind the problem instead of attacking the person. Ask questions to determine what continues to trouble the person about your actions.

Let's evaluate the problem that Jeremiah and Sydney are having.

Jeremiah's point of view: He does not feel appreciated or respected by Sydney. He feels that his wife of ten years talks and treats him like a child. He does not feel that Sydney trusts him, even though he has never given her cause to speculate infidelity. Finally, he feels that Sydney does not believe he is Godly enough because he indulges in a few alcoholic beverages on occasion. Little does Sydney know that on those Friday night outings, Jeremiah has been the designated driver. He will admit that he uses these outings with the guys to remind him that he is useful to someone who appreciates his efforts.

Sydney's point of view: She is so disappointed in Jeremiah. She cannot believe that he would spend more time coordinating his guy-outings than to plan to take her out. He does not spend that much time focusing on things for her. She feels neglected and unwanted. Jeremiah used to take her out for a date night at least once a week. After the children came into the picture, he has had little time to spend with her exclusively. Sydney believes she is rearing the children by herself due to Jeremiah's work schedule. Their sex life is next to non-existent. She feels that maybe he has found someone else to meet his physical needs and that his friends are covering for him every Friday.

Focus people, focus. Focus on the real issue instead of the behavior. Spending time determining where the real problem emanated will keep your mind from wondering in places that are non-productive to the actions of the individual. Sydney moved from a point of disappointment to accusing Jeremiah of infidelity. Jeremiah moved from a point of not being appreciated to avoiding his wife all together. Both places do not promote resolution. Improving your service to one another requires focusing on speaking from a position to be understood instead of focusing on what is being said.

When you focus on what is being said, you are calculating in your mind how to refute and debate a position. Your position must start with assuming innocence. Assuming innocence means that when your spouse states something crazy and out-of-line, that you are ready to ask clarifying questions, instead of the carnal temptation to beat him/her down with their own words. This is not an easy position to take when an argument ensues. You may have to pray in silence while your spouse is speaking, in order to have the right frame of mind. However, consider this - If you actually endure the process to identify the real issue, there is a strong possibility that you can resolve an issue. Imagine moving beyond your circumstances one issue at a time. What a victorious blessing in

184

embracing clarity, reducing conflict through each opportunity to be understood. Praise the Lord!

From a Trifling Act to a Treasured Response: 2 Corinthians 2:14-16

A woman who does not feel protected and respected is considered an uncovered woman. A man who does not feel appreciated and honored is considered a disrespected man.

The first step to recovery:

Husband to wife: Where have I failed to meet your need to be loved and adored?

Wife to husband: Where have I failed to honor and respect you?

Additionally, be prepared to describe to your spouse what your definition of love, adoration, honor and respect looks like. Be prepared to ask these questions without defending the answers you may get. The point of the exercise is not to defend your position. The point of the exercise is to seek out information that can improve your communication with your spouse. The benefits of incorporating clarification and resolution into a relationship have great reward for the spirit and the body. Your marriage becomes the sweet smelling aroma of God working all things out to produce life instead of death.

Special Consideration
This one is for my Single
Brothers and Sisters

Many of the examples within the pages of this book describe in detail, the challenges married couples have experienced because they did not do their homework before walking down the wedding aisle. It is so important that individuals understand the importance of their unique purpose and plan for life before incorporating someone else into that plan and purpose. I want to say the following discussion is written with as much love and kindness as possible. This conversation is not for the light hearted. It is not for the lukewarm or the non-committed Christian.

When you chose to walk as a holy child of God, there are certain expectations that come with the fellowship. Yet many single folks are 'tipping' on the other side of fornication. Don't you realize your behavior will beam like a light from a lighthouse on a foggy night? If you have been lying to yourself, this is your wake up call. Justifying unacceptable behavior will hinder your ability to move in your purpose. Telling yourself that God should be pleased with you because you showed up to church after being out drinking and spending Saturday night in someone's bed is not going to cut it anymore.

Admit it and Quit it. Don't play with God. Don't think you can manipulate God and believe He will continue to cover your trifling behind. God is a God of order. Discipline is necessary to move in the purpose of God. Obedience is HUGE! I have stated previously that the Word of God says that obedience is far better than sacrifice.

Let's take a look at an obedient child of God named Ruth. One of the amazing features that impressed me regarding the relationship with Naomi and Ruth was that Ruth listened and obeyed Naomi. Ruth gave up her own mission to get under Naomi's mission regardless of where that led her.

In this day and age of fast fries, quick oil changes and 'drop it like it's hot', are you willing to listen to an old woman such as myself who says, "Wait on the Lord, believe He will renew your strength daily and will deliver you out of the hands of your oppressor." The truth be told, which is sometimes a challenge for some, if Ruth had failed to follow Naomi's directions exactly, then Boaz would have woken up and found a whore at his feet instead of validating his obligation as a Kinsman Redeemer (*Ruth 2:20*). What do you portray to the world? Just who are you to the kingdom? What do you represent? Where are you going in life? Inquiring minds would like to know!

Point 1: Single on purpose.

It is important for an individual to make a conscious decision to be single instead of being with someone just "to be with someone." Never attempting to learn to be alone with one-self and embrace all of who you are can be dangerous. You don't gain the understanding of who you are- whole by yourself, and

188

not a half waiting for another half to complete you. It is troubling that more and more single people just do not have a strong sense of self-worth. Even if you don't believe you are worth something, consider believing in Jesus who died specifically you. When you walk with God, He will reveal just how unique and precious you are to Him. When you understand how precious you are to God, you will not let any 'breath and britches' tell or treat you otherwise. An individual, who is considered a "breath and britches" type of person, is someone who is only good for sexual pleasure. They have no ambition, goals or desire to be responsible.

Single is your current season in life. Single for a purpose is part of a season God is walking you through right now. In this season identify the purpose God has moved you into. You must recognize that you are in this season so that you can be sensitive to God and what He is saying about and through you. Look internally at those personality traits, behavior patterns and characteristics that God may be perfecting in you. This will allow you to come through this season prepared for the season God is moving you into.

When the Lord brings you out of a "single" season, be advised that God may not immediately deliver you into the hands of someone tall, dark and handsome. Additionally, moving from a single mentality to a married mentality may not result in moving you to your purpose! Getting married cannot be your ultimate goal. After you get married, what are you going to do? Believe it or not, there is life after getting married. The Lord is not going to line you up to what you think you want. God will direct your path to where you need to be. The alternative is that you become disobedient, impatient, and line yourself up with a hot mess, which is not what God designed. Yet, God will convert your mess to work for His glory and your good. When you walk in your own will, God will be with you through the valley when you reap the consequences of your actions. When you are tempted to speed God up remember one thing, at the end of the day God is never late.

Point 2: Mission impossible- Execute patience and maintain your sense of worth

You must execute patience and the tenacity to endure until your purpose and God's plan manifests in the physical. You may observe others that appear to be blessed sooner and faster than you think they deserve. Here is a thought, God knew us before we were formed in our mother's womb (*Jeremiah 4:29*). This being the case, each of you has a unique purpose and plan, which means each of you, will walk in your own unique season.

My season was designed specifically for me. God made each of you unique, so your struggles or lack thereof will be unique as well. This is why the scripture is clear that comparing yourself to someone else is not wise or profitable. Bottom line it is a waste of your time. Concentrate on those things that are good, pleasant, and of good report within yourself.

As you learn to lay aside every weight and sin that so easily besets you that first weight is a lack of self worth. You must learn to respect yourself. If you do not respect yourself you have given others an open invitation to disrespect you. You cannot require

190

something from someone that you do not support yourself.

One of the greatest struggles within the body of Christ is that Christians lose themselves under the misguided premise that they are sacrificing for God. God never told you to forsake who you are in Christ. As a matter of fact the Bible says to love your neighbor as yourself. You are more than your dress size, your breast size and your hip size. You are more than your man, your home and your child. You are greater than your job title, your income bracket and your automobile. You see, none of these will move you into the promises of God- but God and only God with his Word written in your heart will endure forever. When you know you are worth more than gold and silver, you will not let someone beat you, curse at you, or believe the voice of 'player haters'.

Ruth understood the value of living under the anointing of Naomi's wisdom. Ruth's sister-in-law did not appreciate this value. It is really sad that she did not value the sound counsel she was housed under. As long as wine and food is flowing and you're getting your hair done and bills paid by your sugar daddy, life is good. So what if he says you represent his "arm candy" one minute, but he has a "trophy" waiting for him at home.

"Arm candy" is a girl that enhances a guy's physical presentation at parties or other social events. But his true "trophy" is the safe woman at home who had his children, but won't marry her either. You have allowed someone to determine your worth in this life. Terminate with extreme prejudice the notion that you are not complete without a man or a woman. You are only complete through God. No man or woman can be everything all the time in every situation anyway! The concept that you need a man or woman to complete you is to infer that God only made something half way. I seriously doubt that! God did not make half a man and half a woman and then state the two will become one. Two halves make a whole as it refers to fruit, but two halves do not work in a marriage. They just make a whole lot of mess. God designed you to be whole all by yourself.

Point 3: Revelation accompanied with affiliation does not equate to validation of your purpose or your man/woman!

In an effort to help God out, you will seek your own methods to get the "hook up." An individual will surround him/herself with the "right people" in order to validate who they are. They want the right connections, so that they can be at the right place at the right time. However, if your motives are wrong this mentality and behavior will ultimately fail.

Example: You get around a few confident, strong married couples hoping that they will hook you up with someone single. You have made affiliations for the wrong reason and are not in God's order and direction. Slow your roll and work within the revelation God has placed in your spirit that will be revealed in your physical existence.

Take this same scenario and consider what a single individual should glean from a Naomi or Ruth or David or Boaz. Surrounding yourself with strong men and women of God provides an atmosphere that is

192

conducive to learning who you are around some folks that have learned to be comfortable in their own "physical" suit. Someone who is comfortable being who they are is willing to expose themselves in order to encourage and lift you up. Even if that witness is painful to communicate to you, they are willing to take the risk of being seen as "less than" by you so that you can prevent some of the mistakes they have made in the past. This is the type of affiliation that can move you to understand and/or to validate the revelation God has been speaking to you about in the still of the night.

Open a window in your mind to the acquired knowledge of those Godly men and women who just may have a word to say that does not apply to being married, just being whole all by yourself. Instead of stating, "I want what you got" be careful for what you ask. Keep in mind you do not know the cost or price they paid to be in the place where God has them now.

Here is the deal, if the married woman exposes her struggles she has faced and how she overcame them, why in the world would you want to repeat the same experience just to see if she was right or not? That is crazy and not of God. The Bible documents the experiences of individuals who experienced things in order for Christians to know who God is and how He works in their lives.

Just a note, for those of you who are aspiring to be Naomies, be sure you are checking yourself first. Be sure that you pray for direction and guidance before imparting your wisdom. Ensure that you are not ministering through your own pain, through your own stronghold. Just because you have a problem with sex and infidelity does not mean that the person you are ministering to has the same problem. In the same breath, the Ruths of this world should not judge the Naomies of this world by their strongholds. When you study the book of Ruth, Ruth does not bother to address the issue that Naomi changed her name in the middle of Ruth committing her faithfulness to Naomi and God. When Naomi did not believe in herself, Ruth stood in the gap for her mentor.

God is challenging you to look into your own heart and use the gifts He has placed in your hands. As the Lord challenged Moses to use the anointed staff, God is asking you to use the gifts that He has stirred up in you. What do you respect and appreciate about the gift God has given you? If you recognize and respect the gift(s), are you walking in your gift? Or are you too busy chasing some "breath and britches" in the words of Bishop Reams, instead of chasing the call of God on your life? Use your head for more than a hat rack. You are being played by Satan and you have too much to do before God says "well done."

God has stirred up a gift in you that requires your submission to purpose. He reveals your destiny into your spirit. Revelation without application means you just had a good conversation about your situation with God. God will give you the desires of your heart. As you speak to God, your purpose is revealed through the things you are passionate about. I believe I have been called to lift up women of God to know who and whose they are so that when a man does find them; the brother does find a Good Thing! Satan is terrified when you get your direction from God. Satan is satisfied when you let your strongholds get in the way.

Immaturity and Insecurity will hinder your ability to move in your purpose. Immaturity is a lack of knowledge regarding God's Word and how God would have us move in His Word. Insecurity is when you have the knowledge, understand how God works and yet refuse to obey God. Insecurity will paralyze you to move in your purpose. Immaturity is averted by reading God's Word and walking in His promises through faith. Insecurity which consists of unreleased strongholds is freed by confessing your sins to God and walking with a tenacity and strength that only God can provide. Otherwise insecurity will bind you through your fears and hinder your purpose. Learn to seek God's face and hear His voice regarding any insecure and immature behavior in your life.

From a Trifling Act to a Treasured Response: 1 Corinthians 6:19-20

Know you not that your body is the temple of the Holy Spirit? The Holy Spirit within you is the witness of your faith and you are complete in Him. This is why you cannot let Tom or Dick or Harry touch your temple or defile your witness. Your boy that is a friend does not give 'a fornication' about what you believe otherwise he would honor the fact that you believe in celibacy until marriage. You are redeemed with the blood of Jesus. The same power that raised Jesus from the dead sustains you from the devices of the devil. The same power that keeps you from lying and stealing is the same power you call on to resist the spirit of lust in your life. The same power that keeps you from gossiping is the same that combats your proclivity to stay in a depressed state because you are single.

1. Do you have a healthy self image? (Neither inferior nor superior to others).
2. Do you have a possessive spirit as it relates to friends?
3. What have you learned from previous failed relationships?
4. Have you learned to accept constructive feedback?
5. Do you gravitate to unhealthy relationships?
6. List 5 strengths and 5 weaknesses. How do you build on your strengths and manage your weak areas?

Conclusion

You are the "sum total" of all your experiences. Do you want the experiences to change your marriage or do you want to continue with the same trifling acts - going nowhere fast? Are you ready to be set free from the bonds that so easily grip you with the next argument or disappointment from your spouse? I take comfort in knowing that God knows my end from the first breath I took out of my mother's womb. He knew that Darryl and I would develop a great passion for lifting up marriages and dedicate our energy toward that effort. The Lord has anointed, sealed and filled me with His Spirit. Taking hold of God's promises is taking hold of that which God has already given me. The virtuous woman is looking for her king. The king is looking for a Godly woman who will be in awe of his walk with God.

The scripture says that a man who finds a wife finds a good thing. God should find you doing good for your husband. The scripture says that a man should love his wife as Christ loved the church and gave His life for it. God should find you sacrificing your needs for your wife's needs. Only God can give you the tenacity to withstand all the ups and downs of loving and living married.

A trifling fact regarding marriage is that more time is taken planning the wedding then preparing for the marriage. Additionally, the efforts that dominated your strategy to get your spouse must be maintained and stepped up. Your game plan for enhancing your marriage requires a different strategy in order to meet the changing needs of your spouse as you grow up together.

Marriage is not designed for the weak or the feeble minded. God says that when a man marries, he will leave his father and mother and cleave to his wife. (*Genesis 2:24*) The word cleave implies to tackle, to take a strong hold of and possess. This is why a man, who truly loves his wife, should have no problem covering her in all areas. He takes great pleasure in taking hold of what God has entrusted to his responsibility. A wife has no problem submitting to a Godly man, because she knows her husband takes instruction from God not the church and not man. She has a confidence that radiates her covering is God first and her husband second.

Take a vow to walk with God. Make a stand to walk in your purpose and establish goals that line up with that purpose. Many people get purpose and goals confused. Your goals should validate your purpose. For example, if your purpose is to be a witness for Christ, then your goals should line up with being the best witness you can be for the kingdom. Be an example in your own home. Set goals that will show God just how dedicated you are to embracing your spouse. Your purpose can only be validated by the way you walk in life. Don't be trifling and lose track of your purpose in your marriage. This is a trick of the devil to kill, steal and destroy your future.

I leave you with this thought: Marriage is like performing the Waltz with your spouse. **First**: The husband and the wife must have the right posture to stand against the test of time. His left arm should be raised so that the woman's hand can rest lightly in it, and should be held at her eye level. The husband is holding his wife up at all times. The woman, in turn, should rest her left hand comfortably near the man's right shoulder, providing pressure with her fingers and thumb to better "follow" her partner's lead. Your chins must be up. You are watching each other's back as you look purposefully over each other's shoulder.

Second: The husband gently guides his wife into the direction the family should go. If too much force is exerted, your wife will lose her step, causing both of you to fall down. Likewise, the wife must accept the step the husband is taking and move as one body to the music of life.

Third: It takes a great deal of strength for a wife to submit to the direction of her husband. A wife must know just how much pressure to apply to her partner as they dance through a situation. This will prevent her from enabling her husband and encouraging the head of her house to make a move.

Finally: Both husband and wife must maintain a tight bond as they move through this life. That bond is so close that they should be able to hear each other breathing. Holding your spouse close allows you to know and understand the next move your husband or wife is ready to take. This closeness will keep you in step with one another. Prepare for the passion and commitment to return in your marriage by the strength of God.

Matthew 11:12 says that the kingdom of heaven has been forcefully advancing and forceful men lay hold of it. It is time for the men and women of God to forcefully take hold of their marriages. We need to take hold of God's power and advance to enhance our marriages. The devil can no longer assist in the aborting of relationships. God has not given us a spirit of fear, but of love, power and a strong mind. A strong, disciplined mind will challenge what the world says is acceptable in marriage.

No more sleeping around. No more dishonesty. No more deception. Moving from trifling acts to treasured responses requires tenacity, perseverance and commitment to one man and one woman. You can do it! While the examples in this book are accounts of where people failed. Don't stop at the failure! Many of the couples fought back against adversity and restored their marriages. God honored their commitment to restoration. He united with the couples' efforts to build up their relationships. These couples took God at His word and applied His promises to their life. Over time their relationships improved. Yes it will take time and energy, but it is worth it. Take one step at a time and one day at a time.

The scripture says that, "Now faith comes by hearing and hearing by the word of God." Are you ready to walk in the mercy, grace and hope of a "now time" transformation? Now is the time to change how you see your spouse. Now is the time to say "enough is enough". Now is the time to regain the love, passion and trust in your marriage. Now is the time to believe God is a God who can not fail. Fight for what God has given you. Mankind will fail you, but God will never fail nor forsake His children. God ordained marriage. He is counting on you to be a witness through the Holy Spirit that miracles are happening every day through your attitude and actions. The deliverance you can experience in your marriage will be an example of God's glory. **Be Blessed!**

Marriage and the Trifling things we do!